ACTIVATING THE GIFTS OF THE SPIRIT

HANDBOOK

GEORGE PANTAGES

George Pantages Ministries

Evangelist David & Missti Jones

DEDICATION

There are milestones and landmarks in every person's life. The people we meet who come and go throughout our lifetime have the possibility of impacting us so much that our life is never the same. The fine couple this book is dedicated to, David and Missti Jones have had that kind of effect on me. Missti, without being one, is truly my "guardian angel". Since meeting her a couple of years ago my understanding of the use of angels in the miraculous has grown immensely. Although she is so sensitive to the power of angels, she has not let this unique ministry go to her head. One of the great attributes she possesses is her humility. She does not let her gifting get in the way of being submissive to her husband (although when both were in the service, she in the Army and he in the Air Force outranking him) respect for the chain of command keeps her in check. They are the perfect couple in that his strength is in the area of demonology whereas her strength is in angelology.

Missti every once in a while, drops me a text because she can see impending danger before it happens. When we purchased our home a couple years ago (which was abandoned at the time) she warned us of such a danger. When we entered the home for the first time, the door was unlocked, the ceiling fans were on, there was food in the refrigerator, and in actuality someone else was living in the house. When we called the police, they asked us to leave the house while they checked it over. They found both a gun and drugs which could have been used to hurt us. Danger was averted because of the warning she gave us.

I am ever so grateful that the Lord brought them both into our lives to make us more effective in the kingdom of God.

APPRECIATION

I would like to take the time to appreciate the following people for their contribution on the publication of this book:

Michelle Levigne – Editor
Mlevigne.com

Marvin Calderon – Book Cover Design
Mrvn.ECalderon@gmail.com

Adiel Sandoval – Spanish Translation

Maria Pantages – Typesetting

Your professionalism and expertise rang true throughout the entire process, making my writing a whole lot better than it really is.

TABLE OF CONTENTS

GIFTS OF THE SPIRIT: DEFINITIONS & APPLICATIONS..............83

INTRODUCTION

The wisest man who ever lived once said, "There is nothing new under the sun." When we begin to discuss what we believe and how we came to believe them, it is very rare that we have come to our respective beliefs by our own personal study. In reality, most of what we understand as truth has been handed down to us from respected teachers and or people. We have been told what to believe by **not** questioning our authority figures, and out of respect we have fallen into line. At best, we do a lazy, shallow search of the Scriptures to confirm somewhat the truths that have been handed down to us from prior generations. But truth be told, we just follow the status quo and fall into line.

Here are some examples of what I am talking about. Our outward holiness standard, or rather standards differ from state to state and even from city to city. How we dress is predicated upon who is in leadership at that particular time. Is it necessary for both men and women to wear long sleeve shirts and blouses or are short sleeves or sleeveless shirts permissible in this day and age? What about facial hair? For the longest time now, men have been asked to go clean-shaven whereas now many churches are permitting mustaches and beards. The length of hemlines for women have always been at the forefront of our holiness discussions. Is wearing a skirt or dress below the knee modest enough, or do they have to extend to the floor? What about women wearing pants, is that now permissible? Should churches now be able to permit their members to come to service casually dressed or should it always be somewhat formal? Going a bit deeper, what type of worship should we be presenting onto God? Should it be demonstrative and high energy with a controlled chaos dominating our church services or should it remain calm, respectful and low-key? Finally, going even deeper on the spiritual side, what about praying for the sick or praying for someone to receive the baptism of the Holy Ghost? Our custom has been at some point in our worship services, to call up to the altar any sick folk to anoint them with oil believing we have done our due diligence. You should see some of the odd looks I receive when I refuse to use oil to pray for the sick, as if it were a cardinal sin. The problem is, most people are not getting healed and because of that they don't even bother to present themselves before God because in their minds, nothing is going to happen anyway. If we take the time to obey the Scriptures by "healing the sick (Matthew 10:8)" and not just praying for the sick, our results would be far greater than what we are getting at this point.

GIFTS OF THE SPIRIT: IN THEORY

WHERE OUR BELIEFS COME FROM

We have pretty much come to the conclusion that the majority of our beliefs are not from personal Bible study and conviction, but more so from what we have learned from respected teachers. There are two major factors that we use to determine those beliefs: experience and tradition. Let's begin to dissect these factors.

There are several reasons why we don't believe in the miraculous gifts of the Spirit, and one of the greatest reasons is the fact that we have not seen any with our own eyes. If we take a good look into church experiences of today, we cannot find New Testament-quality miracles happening now or even in the history of the church. Many times, there is also the great repulsion caused by the misuse of the gifts in the past that just won't allow everyday Christians to believe God for the miraculous. We are willing to throw out the baby with the bathwater rather than have to put up with misguided, unlearned "prophetic ministries."[1]

Here are some reasons why many don't believe in the miraculous for today's church. In comparing the ministry of Jesus and the apostles when they healed the sick to healing ministries of today, we don't even scratch the surface of how greatly these men of God were used in the past.

When Jesus and/or the apostles healed the sick, the healings were always instantaneous. We find that when the Lord and His apostles were healing the sick, those healings were irreversible and complete. It also appeared that when Jesus and the apostles healed someone, they always seemed to heal the most difficult diseases (i.e., blind, deaf, raising the dead, etc.) We have easily come to the conclusion that Jesus and His apostles could heal at will, under any conditions, and were

---

[1] Jack Deere, Surprised by the Power of the Spirit (Michigan: Zondervan Publishing, 1993) P. 57

always successful as well. On the other hand, when we look at healing ministries today, they are so incomplete. These healings are gradual, sometimes partial, and even at times are reversible. There is this underlying belief that these "ministries" were created to bring wealth to those ministering in that manner, and consequently this leaves a bad taste in our mouth.[2]

How, then, are we to decide what to believe? Should we believe the Christian in today's world is able to duplicate the miracles we read about so frequently in the Bible? Or, was it only for that time, reserved only for the apostles? If we are to gain a complete understanding of what God would want of us in the times we are living today, we need to base our beliefs on the clear and specific teachings of the Scriptures themselves. Tradition, for all the good that it has brought to our lives, must be put aside to release God's glory, allowing Him to move the way His word demands.

---

[2] (ibid. P 58)

DEALING WITH PRESUMPTION

Keep back your servant also from presumptuous sins; Let them not have dominion over me. Then I shall be blameless, And I shall be innocent of great transgression.

(Psalm 19:13)

Definition of presumption: Too confident: done or made without permission, right, overstepping bounds and taking liberties.[3]

PRESUMPTION is not FAITH

Faith is released when God gives us a command and we obey it. Obedience is one of the greatest weapons God has given us to defeat Satan and his minions. Presumption, on the other hand, is nothing more than a good idea that is man-initiated. They are both so similar in practice that it is extremely difficult to tell the difference between the two. To help us understand the concept of Faith vs Presumption,

---

[3] www.merriam-webster.com/dictionary/presuption

we can go to the Scriptures in Matthew 13:24-30 for a clearer picture:

> *"The kingdom of heaven is like a man who sowed good seed in his field; but while men slept, his enemy came and sowed tares among the wheat and went his way. But when the grain had sprouted and produced a crop, then the tares also appeared. So the servants of the owner came and said to him, "Sir, did you not sow good seed in your field? How then does it have tares?" He said to them, "An enemy has done this." The servants said to him, "Do you want us then to go and gather them up?" But he said, "No, lest while you gather up the tares you also uproot the wheat with them. Let both grow together until the harvest, and at that time of harvest I will say to the reapers, "First gather together the tares and bind them in bundles to burn them, but gather the wheat into my barn."*

This parable explains how tares were secretly planted in a wheat field unbeknownst to the owner. Tares look similar to wheat and to try to separate them before the harvest would prove disastrous, because you cannot tell them apart. Only at harvest time do they change enough to be separated from the wheat, but by that time much of the farmer's income is lost. Presumptuous ideas, because they are man-initiated, cannot force God to do something that was not His original idea, no matter how glorious it might sound. Presumption is truly a carnal man's faith!

There is a way that seems right to a man, but its end is the way of death.

(Proverbs 14:12)

I had an experience years ago when I first got converted to the Lord. Shortly after my conversion, I was appointed to be the local youth president. At a district youth meeting, each local representative was given a monthly quota. So as not to be embarrassed by our lack of participation, I decided to put out of my own pocket the quota that was required. I thought I had done a good thing, until shortly after I got called into the pastor's office. He then began to tell me how I had embarrassed him, making him out to be a liar. In shock, I told him I did nothing of the sort. He then told me the rest of the story. He had secretly made an arrangement with the district board to suspend any and all quotas from our local church to the district, explaining that our congregation was too new and too small to comply with district obligations. When the district board saw that the youth department had paid their quota, it made him out to be a liar, totally embarrassing him. What in the beginning started out as a good gesture on my part turned out to be a nightmare. I never again did anything of the sort without consulting him first.

IDENTIFYING PRESUMPTUOUS SINS

If identifying presumptuous sins is essential to living a successful Christian life, then eradicating them is absolutely necessary. So, let's review some false presumptions that hinder our blessings from on high.

Healing was not automatic![4] Jesus could not heal anyone, at any time, in any place, at the drop of a hat.

... And the power of the Lord was present for him to heal the sick.

(Luke 5:17)

If we take the inverse of that Scripture, that means there were times the power of the Lord was not present for Him to heal the sick as well. Again, what Jesus did was not automatic. The next Scriptures bear this out. God heals according to His sovereign will, not human will (PS 72:18; 103:3; 136:4; Exodus 15:26).

---

[4] Jack Deere, Surprised by the Power of the Spirit (Michigan: Zondervan Publishing, 1993 P. 58

Some years back after preaching my message and ministering at the altar, I received a note to pray for a woman who was dying with cancer. I had made up my mind to respond to the request when the Lord stopped me in my tracks. He said, "You can go pray for her if you want to, but I will not heal her." I responded to Him in this manner: "That doesn't sound right to me. Remember, she's dying!" Then the Lord opened up my understanding and said this, "Four weeks ago I gave this woman a chance to be healed. An evangelist visiting this same congregation called her out specifically, stating where the cancer was and that I was willing to heal her instantly. Out of embarrassment to come to the front, she missed out on the opportunity of a lifetime, believing I would give her another chance in the future. I made a decision not to."

Only one man was healed at the pool of Bethesda. This occurrence goes so much against our presumption, believing Jesus will heal anyone, at anytime, anywhere. The pool that day was surrounded by a great number of people in need of healing, but the Lord chose to only heal one man. This is the reason why:

I tell you the truth, the Son can do nothing by Himself; He can do only what he sees the Father doing, because whatever the Father does the Son does.

(John 5:19)

If you believe healing is automatic, why hasn't someone thought of going to all the hospitals, praying for the sick and healing them all? Servants do not actually have a say in what kind of healing takes place. God decides who gets the blessing and directs His servants accordingly. There is a truth that is regularly overlooked in the healing of sick people. They failed to take into consideration that person's will. You can never override a person's will and force them into something they just don't want to do. I will never forget a young lady I met several years ago, who was restricted to a wheelchair because of her inability to walk. During the preliminaries of the service that I would later be speaking in, the Lord revealed to me just how much He wanted to heal her. I stepped down from the platform, excited to share what the Lord had revealed to me. I said, "The Lord has showed me that tonight is the night He will heal you if you so desire." She said something to me that I will never forget: "Please don't pray for me because I do not want to be healed." Stunned by her response, I asked the question anybody would've asked, "Why?" Defiantly she responded, "If God heals me tonight and I am able to walk without the use of this wheelchair, the government will take away the monthly monetary help I receive, and I DO NOT WANT TO WORK!" You can never assume that everyone in need of healing actually wants it. Be that as it may, there has to be an agreement between a person and God for the Lord to do what only He can.

"He could not do any miracles there, except lay his hands on a few sick people and healed them. And he was amazed at their lack of faith..."

(Mark 6:5-6)

Again, I have been sent to particular churches that don't necessarily believe in the miraculous. I remember questioning the Lord as to why I came back when I knew that nothing would happen. His response to me truly floored me when He said,

"I have sent you here to receive a good love offering." I responded, "Lord, You know I don't work that way." He then went on to say this, "Don't worry about it, because they don't listen to Me either." I just laughed to myself!

There is another testimony I'd like to share that speaks volumes as to why someone does not get healed when they are asking for it.

You ask and do not receive, because you ask amiss, that you may spend it on your pleasures.

(James 4:3)

Several years ago while preaching a revival in the state of Texas, a young lady in her early twenties arrived to church in a wheelchair. The first few nights the Lord had led me to pray for people seeking the Holy Ghost and not for healing. What struck me funny was that she never attempted to seek that gift. On the last day of the revival, we arrived at the church about the same time she did. Of course, someone had to drive her to church in a specialized van, and as she made her way to the service you could tell by her body language she was there for one reason and only one reason. She wanted to be healed so she could discard the wheelchair forever. Why? Because the accident took away what she loved the most in life, dancing the night away. When dealing with handicapped people, I try to help them understand the greatest gift God could bestow upon them is not getting physically healed, but rather receiving His spirit and salvation so someday they could make heaven their home. Her bitterness towards God because He had taken away what she had lived for was not going to bring her any closer to receiving her greatest desire. On the last night of the revival, I had encouraged her to seek God's Spirit, but she refused. Because of her bitterness, she left the church that day the same way she had arrived, in a wheelchair, without the ability to walk.

Healing was not automatic for the apostles either...

"*Apart from me you can do nothing.*"

(John 15:5)

I have taken this Scripture to heart and have applied it to my ministry, much to the chagrin of the many people I encounter who I refused to pray for. Because I know healing is not automatic, if I don't receive a specific word from God on how to pray for them and what to do that would connect their actions to the miracle, I am just spinning my wheels. I would rather they be angry at me than at God, so that as they attempt to receive answers in the future, they can be confident that their petitions will be answered accordingly.

Peter made it clear that this power was initiated by the sovereign will of God and only the sovereign will of God.

"Men of Israel, why does this surprise you? Why do you stare at us as if by our own power of godliness we have made this man walk? The God of Abraham, Isaac and Jacob, the God of our fathers, has glorified his servant Jesus."

(Acts 3:12-13)

The apostle Paul confirmed Peter's statement when he also had experiences with his faith not being sufficient to heal the sick. Here are three examples:[5]

1. Paul couldn't heal Epaphroditus:

Yet I considered it necessary to send to you Epaphroditus, my brother, fellow worker and fellow soldier, but your messenger and the one who ministered to my need... For indeed he was sick almost unto death; but God had mercy on him and not only on him but on me also, lest I should have sorrow upon sorrow.

(Philippians 2:25, 27)

---

2. Paul left Trophimus sick at Miletus. Erastus stayed in Corinth, but Trophimus I have left in Miletus sick. (2 Timothy 4:20)

3. Paul exhorted Timothy to take a little wine for his stomach's sake:

---

[5] (ibid. P 63)

No longer drink only water, but use a little wine for your stomach's sake and your frequent infirmities

(1 Timothy 5:23)

Even a special anointing could not guarantee 100 percent success for the apostles see Luke 9:1 and Matthew 10:1

Then He called His twelve disciples together and gave them power and authority over all demons, and to cure diseases.

(Luke 9:1)

With these Scriptures in mind, there was a situation where a father in need of healing for his son went to the disciples for relief. They could not heal the son, so the father made his petition to the Lord.

"Lord, have mercy on my son, for he is an epileptic and suffers severely; for he often falls into the fire and often into the water. So I brought him to your disciples, but they could not cure him." ... Bring him here to Me." And Jesus rebuked the demon and the child was cured from that very hour... "Why could we not cast it out?" ... Jesus said to them, "... This kind does not go out except by prayer and fasting."

(Matthew 17:15, 16, 17, 18, 19, 21)

Before I became diabetic, it was customary for me to go on extended fasts frequently. Depending on the difficulty of the situation that I found myself in, I would fast longer periods of time up to twenty-one days (water only). One day I received my specific instructions to go pray for a lady in our local church who was suffering from stage III cervical cancer. Before I went to do so, I felt led of the Lord to begin an absolute fast for three days to prepare myself. On the evening of the third day, I literally thought I was going to die. Never in my life had I felt such weakness, tiredness, and lethargy, coupled with confusion in my spirit. The confusion was really throwing me for a loop, because in the past, three days of fasting had never affected me so adversely. I was soon to find out why. Nevertheless, I had made up my mind that I would see this time of consecration through, and when I woke up the next morning I found out why. I was scheduled to see the young lady and her husband later in the day, and when I got there the Word of Knowledge kicked in and the Lord began to unfold some problems that were at the root of the debilitating disease. I actually began to minister to the husband first, because it was his unmerciful treatment of his wife that was causing the physical trauma. The cervical cancer was growing rapidly, and if left to run its course, she would die shortly. Of course, the doctors wanted to perform a hysterectomy, which in turn would not allow her to ever bear children, which in her mind was unacceptable. She was between a rock and a hard place. She was dying of cancer, her marriage was falling apart, and she was insecure in her relationship with God. As numb as she was to hear what God had revealed to me about her husband, her reaction to my words floored him. He immediately broke down in tears and asked his wife for forgiveness. Before I laid hands on her, the Lord told me to ask her what she wanted, boy or girl. When she immediately blurted out a little girl, I agreed with her in our prayer and waited for the doctor's confirmation of her healing. Shortly after, our pastor made an announcement that not only was she cancer-free, but she also was pregnant with a little girl! After the time of fasting, God revealed to me why that last day was so traumatizing. I actually stood in her stead, allowing her to live another day to step into her destiny. When impossible situations arise, the only way we can bust through these barriers is through old-fashioned prayer and fasting.

One of the greatest errors in interpreting the Scriptures comes when we erroneously believe that the apostles' healing ministry was the same as the gifts of healing. Let me point out **some** differences.[6]

1. Spiritual gifts vary in their intensity and strength.

   We have different gifts, according to the grace given us... (Romans 12:6)

2. Peter and Paul also had extraordinary healing powers.

---

[6] (ibid. P. 64, 65

"... So that even the handkerchiefs (Paul) and aprons that had touched him were taken to the sick, and other illnesses were cured and these evil spirits left them"

(Acts 19:12)

3. The New Testament presents the apostles as the most gifted individuals within the church. The phrase **signs and wonders (Teras)** is used instead of the term **gifts (Charisma)** to describe their healing ministry. Here are some examples of signs and wonders in the Bible:

- The plagues (Deuteronomy 4:34; 6:22; 7:19; 23:9)
- The ministry of Jesus (Acts 2:22)
- The ministry of the apostles
- The ministry of Stephen (Acts 6:8) and Philip (Acts 8:6)

Signs and wonders are an unusual outpouring of the Holy Ghost where an abundance of miracles are taking place (Acts 5:12; 8:7). Signs and wonders will occur in the midst of revival connected with the proclamation of the gospel.

Summing it up, this is what we have learned:

There is a distinction between signs and wonders and the gifts of healings. Signs and wonders are connected with revival in the proclamation of the gospel, whereas the gift of healing is given to the church for its edification (1 Corinthians 12:7).[7] It is wrong to insist that the apostolic ministry of signs and wonders is the standard for the gifts of healings given to the average New Testament Christian. All we have to do is examine the way God blesses other ministries in the church today. There is no problem believing the statement above in any other ministry. It is time to believe the same when dealing with signs and wonders. Not all of us are great preachers, nor are all teachers profound in our presentations. There are various levels of expertise which we readily accept, so why should this area of ministry (i.e., healing) be any different? We would also have to include those involved in music ministry as well, because again, there are different levels of gifting, whether singing and/or playing an instrument.

---

[7] (ibid. P 66)

We should not draw the conclusion that signs and wonders must have ceased with the death of the apostles. Just because we don't experience them does not mean God does not want to perform them. It happens in the mission field all the time, why can it not to be the same here in the United States?

When we deal in absolutes, it will many times lead to heavy disappointments. Believing that healing is never conditional is one of those erroneous beliefs that has caused so much confusion in the body of Christ. Here are three Scriptures that refute that claim.

"Ask, and it will be given to you; seek and you will find; knock, and it will be opened to you. For everyone who asks receives, and he who seeks finds, and to him who knocks it will be opened."

(Matthew 7:7-8)

The Scripture has been so misunderstood for so long and therefore has brought much confusion to the body of Christ when what has been asked for is not received. I can give you at least two Scriptures that will actually disqualify the Scripture above from being answered by God.

~Surely God will not listen to empty talk (not God's will), nor will the Almighty regard it.

(Job 35:13)

~If I regard iniquity in my heart the Lord will not hear.

(Psalm 66:18)

Asking for things that are "wanted," not necessarily "needed," is not a petition God would waste His time on. Again, Scripture bears this out:

~You ask and do not receive, because you ask amiss, that you may spend it on your pleasures.

(James 4:3)

If you are willing and obedient, you shall eat the good of the land.

(Isaiah 1:19)

I believe most people read this particular Scripture wrongly, and they believe the first part of the Scripture uses the word "or" instead of "and." I say this because in many cases where people are waiting for an answer from God, using one or the other of these words will get them what they are looking for. But in order for the Lord to supply "according to His riches in glory" (Philippians 4:19) a petitioner must be both willing and obedient to receive their answer. Here's a perfect example found in Scripture.

> *...A man had two sons and he came to the first and said, "Go, work today in my vineyard." He answered and said, "I will not," but afterward he regretted it and went. Then he came to the second and said likewise. And he answered and said, "I go, sir," but he did not go.*
>
> *(Matthew 21:28-30)*

Originally the first son refused to go into his father's vineyard, but after a change of heart went out to work. The only difference between him and his brother, who originally told his father he would go and did not, was the fact that it never went any further than lip service. It wasn't until the first son thought about his original response that he took the opportunity to make it right by going to work. At that point, he was both willing and obedient. I know several people who live their lives very much like the second son. They're all talk and no action. Ultimately, these people don't have a clue as to why our heavenly Father does not choose them in the future to labor in His vineyard. Willingness and obedience will always win the prize!

If you confess with your mouth the Lord Jesus Christ and believe in your heart that God has raised Him from the dead, you will be saved.

(Romans 10:9)

I believe this Scripture wholeheartedly, but the door to salvation cannot be opened to anyone until the first step of repentance is taken.

I tell you, no; but unless you repent you will all likewise perish

(Luke 13:3)

The process continues after repentance with water baptism in Jesus' name, according to Acts 2:38, and you shall receive the gift of the Holy Ghost with evidence of speaking in other tongues.

Here is a quick review:

-Confess
-Repent
-Water baptism in Jesus' name
-Receive the Holy Ghost per Acts 2:38

After each step is put into action, salvation has been complete.

SATAN'S DEVIOUS PLAN

Satan's devious trap for every born-again Christian is to substitute faith with presumption. When presumption takes the reins, God is not obligated to answer our petitions because they were never God-initiated, no matter how fantastic the idea may sound. When presumption takes the place of faith, it makes answers to our prayers so unpredictable. We are then so gun shy of stepping out by faith because there is no confidence that the Lord is going to respond to our request, so why go out on a limb when there is no assurance that He will back us up?

And this is the confidence that we have in Him, that, if we ask anything according to His will, He hears us: and if we know that He hears us, whatever we ask, we know that we have the petitions that we desired of Him.

(1 John 5:14-15)

The Scripture above is key to our success in God. Our confidence will always come from praying His will, not ours, and once we know that

He hears us the answer is already on its way. Here are some biblical examples of presumption and how devastating its effects have been on the people of God.

The Scriptures record in Genesis 4:1-8 a classic example of presumption at the highest level. The Lord had asked two brothers, Cain and Abel, to offer a sacrifice unto Him. The sacrifice God had asked for was a blood sacrifice and was to be prepared accordingly. Cain thought he had a better idea and substituted the required sacrifice for a sacrifice of his own choosing. He presumed that if he gave the Lord a sacrifice of what he did best (i.e., grow crops), that that would be as good as if not better than what the Lord was requiring. He presumed that the sacrifice had no spiritual significance, and as long as an offering would be presented to the Lord, that would be enough to pacify Him. He was in total shock when the Lord rejected that sacrifice, and in his bitter reaction to God's rejection he went out and killed his brother. God's rejection of his sacrifice brought to the surface what was really inside of his heart. Cain was not serving God out of love and appreciation. He learned to go with the program, doing just enough to get by.

6° OF SEPARATION

6° of separation[8] is a theory that claims that any person can be connected to another person by no more than six people. Whether Satan uses this system exactly or not, I am positive he uses something similar. This is how it works: Satan is at the top of our adversities, who then orders his top demon in a particular country, who then will order his assistant in a state of that country, who then orders the top demon in charge of the city, who then orders the demon in charge of a local church, who then influences you without you knowing this person has been sent from hell.

6° OF SEPARATION

SATAN
USA
CALIFORNIA
LOS ANGELES
LOCAL CHURCH
YOU

[8] www.urbandictionary.com/define

If Satan's covert operations are so strategic and almost undetectable, how in the world will we be able to avoid presumptuous errors? We must adhere to the word of God and not our emotions. The word will guide us regardless of circumstances and negative outcomes. Looking at the word and not our circumstances will keep our minds in perfect peace.

You will keep him in perfect peace, whose mind is stayed on You, because he trusts in You.

(Isaiah 26:3)

This clever maneuver has been used effectively when the church presumes a certain understanding of Scripture handed down from previous generations, without understanding the full impact the Scripture could have on our lives if we will just dig a little bit deeper. For example, look at Romans 10:17 a moment.

So then faith comes by hearing, and hearing by the word of God.

So many children of God have believed a half-truth that becomes a stumbling block in understanding the concept of faith. Many of us have been taught that when a formidable challenge is set before us, to immediately go to the word and find a Scripture you can stand on by faith until God gives you the victory. As many times as people have used this approach to find their answers, most of the time it doesn't work. That's the reason why many people lose hope in extending their faith, abandoning it completely because they fail more than succeed, and that my friend is utterly frustrating. Where have we gone wrong? We have failed to understand that the apostle Paul does not use in Romans 10:17 the common word for "word," which is translated logos. Paul chooses instead to use the word rhema. Now then, logos can at times be rhema, but not always. Logos is the written word of God, whereas rhema is the spoken word of God. The best definition of rhema I have ever heard is this one: rhema is "a specific word, for a specific person, for a specific situation." A specific word given to us that launches our faith into the miraculous, a journey we will have to travel by ourselves with no outside help from others. It is what causes truly obedient people to be misunderstood because there is no rhyme or reason to explain the things that God is leading us to do.

THE ENCHILADA GUY

Here is one of my "eccentric" examples:

In 2017, we were ministering in the state of Washington during the week in a tiny congregation. They were responding very well to the word, but what caught my attention was one particular woman who would respond to everything I said with exuberant laughter. It just so happened that after the service she approached me with a petition for her husband. She said, "I would like to ask prayers for my husband because at the moment he is hospitalized. Tomorrow, the doctors have to make a decision whether they will amputate his foot or not. I'm asking that the Lord would heal him." I have learned from experience not to "lay hands suddenly" (1 Timothy 5:22) without finding the root of the problem. Initially when I received my instructions, I rejected them as being a trick of Satan. This is what I was impressed to say, "After service tonight, go visit your husband in the hospital and serve him a plate of enchiladas. He will be fine in the morning!" Now then, I can find Scripture to support the use of oil to heal the sick

(James 5:14) but enchiladas? I then took a step of faith and just blurted it out. Immediately she broke out in raucous laughter, which ended with, "I can do that." When the service was over and I had an opportunity to speak to my wife, I told her we needed to leave the hotel the next morning early enough to escape the ridicule I anticipated receiving. The next morning before checkout I received a text message with a photo. It started off with this: "Just to let u know on the enchilada guy?" I was afraid to read the rest of the text, but lo and behold, in his hospital gown was a man devouring a plate of enchiladas. The rest of the text said that after waking up the next morning he was checked again, and to the amazement of the doctors he was completely healed and the procedure was called off!

Just to let u know on the enchilada guy... got this text "DID YOU HEAR PASTOR ! PATS FOOT IS STAYING ON !!! THERE IS NO BACTERIA AT ALL IN THE FOOT ! 😃

Obedience to God's instructions will always bring positive results no matter how outlandish they may appear. A specific word, for a specific person, for a specific situation, is just how God rolls. Now, for those of you thinking that I have received a new revelation in praying for the sick, think again. I was foolish enough to think that myself, so I tried to apply this rhema to my own life. When gangrene had set in on one of my toes shortly after the "enchilada experience," I thought it would be a good idea to go to the nearest Mexican restaurant and order a plate of enchiladas to receive my healing. Well, sad to say, it didn't work. God has several ways He can supply our needs. There is no need to memorize a particular act we followed the last time we asked Him for a miracle, because chances are if we are in a similar situation, He will choose another avenue to bless us to keep us on our toes.

THE PRESUMPTION OF KING SAUL

This next example of presumption clearly shows how good intentions are not good enough to override God's laws.

Then he (King Saul) waited seven days, according to the time set by Samuel. But Samuel did not come to Gilgal; and the people were scattered from him. So Saul said, "Bring a burnt offering and peace offerings here to me." And he offered the burnt offering. Now it happened, as soon as he had finished presenting the burnt offering, that Samuel came; and Saul went out to meet him, that he might greet him. And Samuel said, "What have you done?" Saul said, "When I saw that the people were scattered from me, and that you did not come within the days appointed and that the Philistines gathered together at Michmash, then I said, 'The Philistines will now come down on me at Gilgal, and I have not made application to the Lord.' Therefore I felt compelled, and offered a burnt offering." And Samuel said to Saul, "You have done foolishly. You have not kept the commandment of the Lord your

God, which he commanded you. For now the Lord would have established your kingdom over Israel forever. But now your kingdom shall not continue...

(1 Samuel 13:8-14)

We find King Saul between a rock and a hard place. He had prepared his army to do battle, and the only thing needed to begin was to make a sacrifice unto the Lord that would secure the victory. As he waited and waited and waited, Samuel the prophet who would make the sacrifice was nowhere to be found. The king presumed that since there was no one of authority to make that sacrifice, he himself would take responsibility of sacrificing unto the Lord. A good idea perhaps, but on the other hand unlawful. In those days, only priests or prophets could offer sacrifices. That day the king sadly found out that the end does not justify the means. He honestly believed that sacrificing without authority would be overridden by the need. How could God reject a spiritual work that was needed to go into battle? When the prophet rebuked Saul, the king was surprised by the rebuke. In his eyes, he had done a good thing, and if anything he should have been praised for taking the reins of a bad situation and making it right. When a person is not in line with the word of God and His commandments, judgment upon him will always come as a surprise. Never in his wildest imagination did he think he would be judged for doing a good work. Presumptuous people never see the entire picture, only what is in their best interests, which many times does not include the will of God. It was this act of disobedience that caused Saul to lose his kingdom and ultimately lose his life. Presumptuous people never have a clue as to why God rejects their good works, because they live by their emotions and emotions are deceitful.

The heart is deceitful above all things, and desperately wicked; Who can know it?

(Jeremiah 17:9)

THE PRESUMPTION OF EVE

Satan will try to disguise presumption, and believe me, he is a master at it. One of his greatest weapons is to take God's word out of context and twist its meaning to negate the promise we will be standing on. This was Eve's mistake in the Garden of Eden when the serpent challenged God's word. Her presumption overrode her obedience to the Lord, and it opened the door to sin.

Then the serpent said to the woman, "You will not surely die. For God knows that in the day you eat of it your eyes will be opened, and you will be like God, knowing good and evil." So when the woman saw that the tree was good for food, that it was pleasant to the eyes, and a tree desirable to make one wise, she took of its fruit and ate. She also gave to her husband with her, and he ate.

(Genesis 3:4-6)

Never could Eve have imagined the consequences of her sin being so harsh. Not only would childbearing from that day forward be so painful, but even more devastating was the fact that she no longer had equal authority with her husband Adam. Her name was instantly changed from Adam to Eve:

Male and female created he them; and blessed them, and called their name Adam, in the day when they were created.

(Genesis 5:2 KJV)

It was then that she became a second-class citizen, being placed under his rule and authority. Now it makes so much more sense as to why women in general have such a disdain to be ruled by a man. It was part of Eve's judgment in the garden and it continues even today. Truly this Scripture below takes on more significance when we realize its truth.

... Behold, to obey is better than sacrifice...

(1 Samuel 15:22)

SATAN'S PRESUMPTUOUS ERROR

Satan was counting on the Lord being presumptuous when in the wilderness he tempted Him three times. He began the temptation by appealing to His hunger and bodily weakness.

Now when the tempter came to him, he said, "If You are the Son of God, command that these stones become bread." But He answered and said, "It is written, 'Man shall not live by bread alone, but by every word that proceeds from the mouth of God.'"

(Matthew 4:3-4)

When Jesus did not bite, he attacked Him in another way, appealing to His flesh.

And said to Him, "If You are the Son of God, throw Yourself down. For it is written: 'He shall give His angels charge over you,' and, 'In their hands they shall bear you up, lest you dash your foot against a stone.'"

(Matthew 4:6)

Finally, when those two temptations had no success, he proceeded to appeal to Christ's purpose.

Again, the devil took Him up on an exceedingly high mountain, and showed Him all the kingdoms of the world and their glory. And he said to Him, "All these things I will give You if You will fall down and worship me." Then Jesus said to him, "Away with you, Satan! For it is written, 'You shall worship the Lord your God, and Him only you shall serve.'"

(Matthew 4:8-10)

Again, a failed effort by the enemy. The word always has an answer for whatever opposition comes our way.

MAKING A PARADIGM SHIFT

Definition of a Paradigm: A theory or a group of ideas about how something should be done, made, or thought about.[9]

One of the greatest challenges in the church today is making paradigm shifts without creating a chaotic mess. I say that because even the smallest of changes (i.e., moving the piano from one side of the platform to the other) can ruffle a lot of feathers, causing negative responses that are not easily repaired. Time and time again, I have heard horror stories recounted by new pastors taking over an existing church that had been established for many years, with a congregation that believed their way of running a church was the only way a church should be managed, including worshiping God. In their view, the founding fathers were led by God to do things a certain way, and any change from that was considered blasphemy. There is no room for visionary leadership because that would only mean that this new generation was watering down the gospel, and truth cannot be changed. It is very difficult for them to distinguish the differences between truth and tradition, so to be on the safe side, everything stays the same.

---

[9] www.merriam-webster.com/dictionary/paradigm

This paradigm shift I would like to share is one that almost caused our local church to be kicked out of our church organization. What was the change that caused such a ruckus? We were one of the first churches in our Spanish organization to raise a church that spoke entirely in English. The negative response was so overwhelming it made our pastor second-guess himself, even to the point he thought about leaving the organization to fellowship in one that would allow us the liberty to worship God in the only language we spoke. It was only when the former president of our organization defended our pastor that we were allowed to continue doing what we were doing without repercussions. He was a man who only spoke Spanish, nevertheless he had enough wisdom to understand that a new Hispanic generation was being raised in the United States without speaking one word of Spanish. From that day forward, any time he was in the area, he had carte blanche to come speak in our church any time he wished. The funny thing about it was, as he would preach to us even though we did not understand a word he said, we would respond with the only word that we knew in Spanish, which was "Amen."

What was the result of our pastor's audacity? We grew from a starting congregation of twelve to about close to 600 members in its heyday. Although criticism from our district continued, it was hilarious to see so many young people from other churches in our area visiting our Friday night services, sent by their pastors to receive the Holy Ghost. We were then one of the first churches to start a K-12 Christian school, which eventually became a "Model School" in the ACE program. The boys' basketball team, if I am not mistaken, won six straight state championships. The education department then branched out to open a daycare for preschoolers. Our church choir became renowned in winning countless awards, but what we really hung our hat on was the drug rehabilitation program (Lifeline Outreach) that became the pillar of our success. Only a visionary like our pastor, Rev. David Hernandez, saw that and never let opposition to these visions stop him from doing the will of God.

I can imagine the looks on the faces of the apostles when Jesus made a paradigm shift when celebrating the Passover.

And as they were eating, Jesus took bread, blessed and broke it, and gave it to the disciples and said, "Take, eat; this is my body." Then He took the cup, and gave thanks, and gave it to them, saying, "Drink from it, all of you. For this is My blood of the new covenant, which is shed for many for the remission of sins.

(Matthew 26:26-28)

Probably up to that point, most of them weren't even paying attention because they had this ceremony memorized to the very last word. When Jesus took the rituals of the Passover, using them to rename this event to the Last Supper, I am sure it raised a lot of eyebrows as His disciples looked on. The ritual itself was not being changed, only the meaning of it.

I believe an event that came close to this shock was when the Lord called Peter to take the gospel to the Gentiles for the first time. Talk about paradigm shifts! The Spirit of God really had to go out of His way to help Peter understand the enormity and importance of his next assignment.

...Peter went up on the house top to pray, about the sixth hour. Then he became very hungry and wanted to eat; but while they made ready, he fell into a trance and saw heaven opened and an object like a great sheet abound at the four corners, descending to him and let down to the earth. In it were all kinds of four-footed animals of the earth, wild beasts, creeping things, and birds of the air. And a voice came to him, "Rise, Peter; kill and eat." But Peter said, "Not so, Lord! For I have never eaten anything common or unclean." And a voice spoke to him again the second time, "What God has cleansed you must not call common." This was done three times and the object was taken up to heaven again.

(Acts 10:9-16)

When the servants of Cornelius shortly after this event came knocking at his door requesting his presence, Peter finally began to put two and two together. He made a great paradigm shift, neglecting what he had been taught for the new revelation Christ was bringing to his understanding. He then accepted the invitation of these Gentiles to preach to Cornelius for the first time the Acts 2:38 message. Not only did this Gentile man and his family receive the oneness message, being baptized in water in Jesus' name, they also received the baptism of the Holy Ghost, speaking in other tongues as the Spirit of God gave the utterance.

What Peter never took into consideration, when trying to understand what the vision meant, was the fact that Jesus had already changed the law of the Jews when He declared this statement in Mark 7:18-19:

> So He said to them, "Are you thus without understanding also? Do you not perceive that whatever enters a man from outside cannot defile him, because it does not enter his heart but his stomach, and is eliminated, thus purifying all foods?"

In essence, what Jesus was saying in this statement was that He was making and declaring all food ceremonially clean, that is, abolishing all the ceremonial distinctions of the Levitical law. Christ's death on Calvary sealed the deal!

DISRUPTING OUR VISION

Satan's main objective is to steer us off course by disrupting our vision. The greatest definition of sin that I have been able to apply to my own life is this:

SIN = "MISSING the MARK." Satan doesn't necessarily have to lead you into gross sin, he just wants to steer you off course enough to keep you from your destiny. When our vision has been disrupted by missing the mark, it has robbed us from a full understanding of what FAITH really is. Let me put it in these terms. When I suffered my stroke and heart attack in 2013, one of the many issues I had to deal with was what the doctors call a neglect in my eyesight. Basically, what that boils down to is this: although I can see clearly with both eyes, my peripheral vision in my right eye has been taken away. It is serious enough to convince my wife not to allow me to drive anymore because although I believe I have complete vision in my right eye, it is not actually true. There are times when my lack of peripheral vision does not allow me to see people approaching me from my right side. It causes a lot of harrowing moments, because they suddenly appear out of nowhere and scare me half to death.

When I am in a place where there are a great number of people, I find it very challenging not to be bumping into them because there is no peripheral vision to help safeguard me. That being said, this same concept applies to our spiritual lives as well. I am sure that any pastor with any kind of experience in counseling would agree with the next statement I will make. How many times have you counseled others hearing them say this: I just don't see it that way, Pastor. It's not a physical neglect of the eyes that is causing problems for them understanding, it is more so a spiritual neglect. Our leaders can see things in our lives more profoundly than we can, when in reality we don't have a clue.

LOSE AN EYE OR DIE

There is an excellent example of vision being disrupted in the Old Testament in 1 Samuel 11. Israel was being surrounded by the armies of Nahash, threatening to destroy them. Nahash promised not to destroy them if they would agree to his one and only condition. They had to let him gouge out the right eye of each Israeli soldier.

"On this condition I (Nahash) will make a covenant with you, that I may put out all your right eyes, and bring reproach on all Israel."

(1 Samuel 11:2)

Losing a right eye was nothing compared to losing a life, so on the surface it appeared to be a win-win situation. What the casual observer does not understand is that the loss of the right eye would completely and permanently cripple any soldier in Israel's army from fighting the enemy for the rest of their life. Because their shields protected their entire body less the right eye, it was the only body part they could not afford to lose if they were to be successful in battle. Without the use of the right eye, Israel was completely defenseless.

The most effective weapon Satan has in his arsenal is the use of half-truths. Like in the example above, when Satan used a half-truth to convince Eve to eat of the forbidden fruit, this weapon used is downright deceitful. The best scriptural example I can use that is deceitful is found in Romans 10:17:

So then faith comes by hearing and hearing by the word of God.

For generations we have restricted the effectiveness of this scripture as stated earlier in the book by limiting its definition of "word" to the Greek word logos (the written word of God). The problem is, in this case "word" is translated rhema, which not only includes the written word but the spoken word as well. How does this affect our decision-making? There are times that the written word will not have a specific answer for the situation we find ourselves in. It is then and only then the spoken word will bring us the answers we are looking for. The best definition of rhema I have found is this one: **A specific word, for a specific person, for a specific situation.** This definition will not only bring clarity to difficult situations, it also helps to avoid presumptuous decisions before lives are destroyed.

The following testimony is one of my favorite examples I use to explain what a rhema word is:

Years ago, a young man was sent out to pastor a church that was a graveyard for pastors. No matter who was sent, how long they stayed, the result was always the same, utter failure. When this new pastor arrived, like the others, he was bright-eyed and bushytailed. He was going to do there what nobody else could in the past. Sad to say, after a short period of time, it didn't appear that he would be successful as well. One day in prayer, the Lord spoke to him with these specific instructions, "Change the times when you hold Sunday night services to midnight, and you will have revival." When this message was first received, the pastor could not discern whether this was from God or not. If it wasn't, what did he have to lose, because no one else had been able to bring revival to this town either. But if it was God, something so unlikely would be a part of his success, and of course God would get all the honor and glory. Shortly thereafter, he made the change, and lo and behold, the greatest revival that congregation had ever experienced broke out. People were getting saved by the hundreds, God confirming this move by also filling them with the Holy Ghost. The following year when General Conference came along, news of this great revival had spread like wildfire, and other young pastors wanted to know what he had done to be so successful in such a short period of time.

"You wouldn't believe me if I told you," he said.

"Come on, man. Don't hold out on us, we really need to know."

"Like I told you before, even if I was willing to tell you, it is unlikely you would believe me anyway."

"You let us be the judge of that, just tell us."

"Just remember, I told you, you won't believe me. I changed the hours I have service on Sunday evenings to twelve midnight, because that is what God told me to do."

"You really expect us to believe that cockamamie story?"

He responded to their unbelief, "I told you so." Because this young pastor had received a specific word, for a specific person, for his specific situation, it was enough for him to branch out by faith and let God handle the rest.

WHY GOD DOESN'T HEAL

That is something I believe most people would like to know, and rightfully so. An absence of signs and wonders amongst God's people usually means divine judgment has fallen upon them.

We do not see our signs; There is no longer any prophet; Nor is there any among us who knows how long. Oh God, how long will the adversary reproach? Will the enemy blaspheme Your name forever? Why do you withdraw Your hand, even Your right hand? Take it out of Your bosom and destroy them.

(Psalm 74:9-11)

Look how Israel reacted to the punishment God was allowing them to experience, basically to open their eyes to their folly. It was necessary, because as a whole, they were a very stiff-necked people and needed harsh discipline to come to their senses. God's presence had been hindered by their backslidden lifestyle, so He removed it along with His protection.

Another reason why God doesn't heal is because of two conditions that have crept into our lives and have dominated our walk with Him. When legalism rears its ugly head, it leads to lukewarm faith. This in turn causes a disconnect with heaven.

> *For the Lord has poured out on you the spirit of deep sleep, and has closed your eyes, namely, the prophets; and He has covered your head, mainly, seers.*
>
> *(Isaiah 29:10)*

Here is a testimony I mentioned earlier but in more detail that happened early in my experience with God that I will never forget. When my uncle, who eventually became my pastor, graduated from Bible school, he returned to our area to open a new church. There was a group of about twelve, and slowly but surely the church began to grow. We found out shortly after that the district officials were distraught and not in agreement with how the pastor was running the church. Were we preaching false doctrine? Were we lowering our standards in any way? No, not really. What they were disagreeing with was the fact that all our services were in the English language. At that time, our organization was about 95 percent Hispanic, which meant all services were ministered in Spanish. The meeting was held to determine whether we could continue ministering in English or if not, be asked to leave the organization. On the day of that meeting, unexpectedly, one of the pioneers of the organization walked in the meeting unannounced. As the officials began to explain the situation and what, in their eyes, needed to be done, this man of God asked permission to speak.

He said, "You know that I do not speak a word of English and I really don't understand why someone believes he could grow a church using another language than what we are accustomed to. But, on the other hand, if God has spoken to him to do this and we do not permit him to do so, then we are fighting against God. It is my suggestion to leave him be, because if this is of God, we will not be able to stop it. On the other hand, if this is not of God, what are you afraid of? It will all fall apart, and he will not have to fault us for his lack of success."

After this wise word of counsel, a vote was taken, and we were allowed to stay. In the aftermath, the church began to grow like wildfire. Our Friday night services were so impactful that many of the other churches in the district would send their young people to get them fired up. In its heyday, this church grew to about 600, and what our pastor was doing to bring revival to our church was then copied by the rest of the churches in the district.

A legalistic point of view will circumvent God's perfect will in our lives to the point that we will always be found in a lukewarm state, one which God literally hates. The ministry of signs and wonders will be nipped in the bud because God will not tolerate one of His children being lukewarm.

So then, because you are lukewarm, and neither cold nor hot, I will vomit you out of My mouth.

(Revelation 3:16)

If legalism and being lukewarm head the list of reasons why God will not heal, unbelief has to be a close second.

And he did not many mighty works there because of their unbelief.

(Matthew 13:58)

Perhaps the most difficult place to work in the miraculous is when you are amongst friends and family. Jesus verified this in Mark 6:4 when He said:

But Jesus said to them, "A prophet is not without honor except in his own country, among his own relatives, and in his own house."

I so identify with this last statement, because when I go back to the church I was saved in, those who knew me back then have a difficult time accepting this new change in ministry. Why? Because it has been a complete about face. In His mercy, the Lord does permit some healings and miracles, but it usually happens to those who are new to the church and did not know me back then.

THE REDEMPTIVE VALUE OF SUFFERING

The last reason God does not heal is perhaps the most important and yet the most rejected because of the pain involved. There is a great redemptive value in suffering, so much so, its effectiveness is far above any of the other methods God uses to draw us closer to Him.[10]

And He said to me, "My grace is sufficient for you, for My strength is made perfect in weakness." Therefore most gladly I will rather boast in my infirmities, that the power of Christ may rest upon me.

(2 Corinthians 12:9)

No one really knows what the thorn in Paul's flesh was. It could have been an illness or perhaps a type of persecution. Whatever the case was, God chose not to remove it. Countless times in my own life physical issues have hindered me in ministry. Initially, I would ask the Lord to remove them, because in my mind I could be far more effective without the various pains and

---

[10] Jack Deere, Surprised by the Power of the Spirit (Michigan: Zondervan Publishing, 1993) P. 155

weaknesses that rack my body constantly. I actually stopped asking for one particular healing of my body when the Lord revealed to me why He considered it best not to.

After being miraculously healed of polio at the age of five, some years later my mom told me the rest of the story. I was nearing death, like most of the children in my ward who eventually died of this dreaded disease. One day my grandfather came to my mom, encouraged by a dream he had had. He said, "Daughter, the Lord has showed me that Junior (me) was going to be healed." She was somewhat skeptical, because every day as she visited me after work, I almost always had a new companion in my room. Unbeknownst to me, my roommates were dying every day.

The thought that my day was coming soon was terrifying her, more so because at that time she was not living right for God. As much as she wanted to believe her father for a miraculous healing, she felt she was unworthy and that this situation was brought about by her unfaithfulness to Him. He then said this to her, "When God heals him, the sign for you will be everything will be normal in his body except for a withered right arm." A little bit later, she received that dreaded call to come because chances were, I would not make it through the night. With a little bit of faith, she called our pastor. He prayed a short prayer, and shortly afterward I was released from the hospital. On the way out, the doctor who attended to me stopped my mom in the hallway and said this, "Mrs. Pantages, we don't know what God you serve, all we know is that the healing of your son did not come from modern medicine. Your God has answered your prayers, and this is a verified miracle."

Every day in my struggles to do the things that other people don't even think twice about, I go back to that day and am ever grateful for the mercy that the Lord showed to me. There truly is redemptive value in suffering, because I have been able to use this experience in my ministry dealing with other folk who are hurting just as much as I did, if not more so. I've seen God miraculously heal blinded eyes, unstop deaf ears, and heal people stricken with cancer who had no hope from modern medicine. They left the church that day cancer-free after a short, faith-filled prayer. The doctors were able to verify this later. I have observed barren women leave encouraged, knowing that the baby they had been asking God for was on its way, and found out later on that it did come to pass exactly the way God said it would. Does it make my struggles physically any less? Not by a long shot, but every time I have the opportunity to look at this weak, withered, lifeless arm and hand, it gives me another chance to lift my hands and raise my voice to the God who has showed His mercy to me and give Him the honor and glory He rightfully deserves.

GIFTS OF THE SPIRIT: DEFINITIONS & APPLICATIONS

For to one is given by the Spirit the word of wisdom; to another the word of knowledge by the same Spirit; To another faith by the same Spirit; to another the gifts of healing by the same Spirit; To another the working of miracles; to another prophecy; to another discerning of spirits; to another divers kinds of tongues; to another the interpretation of tongues

(1 Corinthians 12:8-10) KJV

The definitions I will be using are borrowed from my mentor Evangelist Freddy Clark, with his permission.

THE 9 GIFTS OF THE SPIRIT

SIX SENSES OF THE SPIRIT

In order to get a full understanding of how the gifts of the Spirit work, it is imperative to understand how our five senses work in the spiritual realm. The five senses (in the Spirit there are six) work very similar to the ones God physically gave us. Let's review each one:

- See
- Hear
- Feel
- Taste
- Smell
- Know

Now let's take each one of the senses individually to explain how they work in the Spirit.

When a person is gifted to see things in the Spirit, it is very similar to a video presentation. You can pretty much describe in detail what is going on in the spiritual realm. People who work in this area have told me that it is actually viewed in living color. Here's a good example: a good friend of mine who is highly gifted received a vision, which, if he was wrong, could possibly have both his license and his pastorate taken away from him. While in a district service, the Lord revealed to him an adulterous affair his district superintendent was having. That's a pretty heavy accusation to place upon a man of God who was highly respected. My friend tried to play it off as being his own imagination, but the Lord would not let it go. He then asked the Lord that if what he was feeling was true, to give him a sign that would lift his faith to bring it out in the open. The Lord then gave him a vision right before his eyes in a way that he could not deny what he had been feeling in his spirit. All of a sudden, he was told to focus on a particular woman in the congregation, and with that he began to see what appeared like a serpent beginning to slither up and around that woman's body, eventually covering her from head to toe. Confident now that what he was sensing was true, he had to go to the next step to reveal this hidden sin to the higher authorities. Because that man had such an impeccable testimony of faithfulness in all facets of life, of course this accusation could not be backed up with any kind of evidence. A meeting was set up to allow the accused to defend himself and nip the allegation in the bud before it spread out of control. As expected, he denied the entire accusation as a farce. The accused woman then had her opportunity to confirm what the superintendent had testified to, or of course confess to the alleged affair. She vehemently denied it. My friend would not back down because the impressions he had received began to get stronger, but it looked like without any kind of proof he was going to take the fall for the supposed false accusations. Totally humbled by this experience and then humiliated by his superiors, as depressed as he had become, the Lord encouraged him to continue to pray. From one day to the next, the conviction of the accused woman would not let her sleep and she finally confessed that the accusations were true. Even then, the district superintendent denied her confession and called her a flat-out liar. Long story short, he eventually humbled himself, confessed to the sin, and his position was taken away.

There is another testimony I would like to share, more on the lighter side. When it came time to give money to his children, my dad loved to play games. There was one particular time when I tried to collect from him money he had promised. He playfully checked his pants pockets, both front and back, and there was no wallet to be found. My dad was always impeccably dressed, meaning wherever you would find him he would be wearing a nicely tailored suit. It was then that the Lord revealed to me that the wallet was in the inside pocket of his suit coat, the left pocket to be exact. I then said to him, "Dad, check the inside pocket of your coat on the left side and you will find your wallet." With a look of unbelief, he then began to laugh and the playful look on his face told me he had just been caught. Thank God for revelation!

The next sense is that of hearing in the Spirit. Up to this point in my personal experience with God, I have not heard the audible voice of the Lord, nor do I know anyone who has. Of course, I have read and heard at various times about people who have, so I do believe God uses our hearing to speak to us audibly if the need arises. The biblical account I would like to share is that of Samuel.

We find in 1 Samuel 3:3-9 an account when the Lord was beginning to speak to Samuel personally, without him initially understanding what was going on. Two times he got up and went before Eli, and the man of God sent him back to sleep, telling him he did not call. On the third time, Eli sent him back with specific instructions:

Therefore Eli said to Samuel, "Go, lie down; and it shall be, if He calls you, that you must say, 'Speak, LORD, for Your servant hears.'" So Samuel went and lay down in his place. Now the LORD came and stood and called as at other times, "Samuel! Samuel!" ...

(1 Samuel 3: 9-10)

It is such a great example to know that the Lord will call upon anyone sensitive and obedient enough to respond to His voice, regardless of age, experience, or gender.

To be able to feel or sense things in the Spirit is one of the most common ways God speaks to us. I know of many evangelists who, when praying for the sick, begin to feel in their body the area of pain people are suffering from as they stand before them. When I initially found out that God used this method to help heal the sick, I pleaded with Him that if there were another way to be successful in a healing ministry without having to suffer any more pain, to please allow me to use that way instead. If you know me personally, you would know that from the time I was five years old, suffering with polio, my life has always been a plethora of weakness in my body. My gifting then is more on the knowing level, which I will discuss a little bit later in more detail.

Here are a few examples that I have heard over the years of how the sense of feeling is used. There was a particular man of God whose greatest gift of healing dealt in the area of cancer. What allowed him the utmost confidence in calling out to the audience folks he believed were suffering with cancer, was a particular sign God used when the Lord wanted to heal a person or persons in that particular meeting. Without warning, out of the blue, the palms of this man of God would begin to burn as if they were on fire. This was God's way of letting him know what He desired to do that day. It was a sign unique to his ministry, a sign that brought miraculous healing of a disease that has continued to kill millions.

As far as tasting in the Spirit, I can only refer to a common experience that happens to my mentor, Evangelist Freddy Clark. He will actually begin to taste tobacco in his mouth to confirm that the person he is ministering to has a problem with smoking. As soon as that person confesses to that problem, he prays for them, and when the Lord delivers them from that habit, the taste in his mouth goes away.

The next sense is that of smell. Very similar to the example above of tasting tobacco when a person has a problem with it, in my case I can smell it on them even if they have not smoked in weeks. Again, after prayer and God delivers them, I do not smell that odor anymore. But, the best example I can give of smelling in the Spirit is something that happened to me years ago that had a profound effect in my ministry.

AN EXPERIENCE I WILL NEVER FORGET

I was praying for people at the altar in a particular service, making my way from one end of the building to the other. As I approached the other side, the closer I got to a certain man praying, a stench so foul emanated from him that it almost made me vomit. I was determined to pray for him anyway, when the Lord stopped me in my tracks. What I found strange was that he was surrounded by others praying and no one else seemed to be bothered by what I was smelling. The Lord helped me to understand that His judgment had fallen upon this man and He was not going to heal him. Immediately after the service, I received a note to meet that same man in a private place. We went to an empty Sunday school room and he began to unfold a story that I needed to hear.

He said, "I admire your zeal for God and how the Lord uses you. I identify so much, because at one time I had a similar ministry. To tell you the truth, it was far more advanced than yours." I began to wonder why in the world he was telling me all this. The Lord then whispered to me to listen to what he had to say, so I let him continue. He went on to say this, "My ministry began to grow in leaps and bounds, traveling all over the country. My calendar was always full and I lacked for nothing financially. There came a time that I was in such demand that I would overbook myself because of the pride that had grown unchecked. I found out something about ministering in the Spirit that eventually became my downfall. In times when I barely had enough time to get off the plane into church, there were times that I did not pray, and it appeared in those times that God used me more powerfully than in times I consecrated myself before ministering. I began to rationalize that my prayer life wasn't that essential to be used in the manner that I was accustomed to, so little by little I let go of my consecrated life. It was then that seducing spirits overwhelmed me, and I eventually fell into sin, committing adultery on a one-night stand. Sad to say, I was stricken with AIDS and now I am dying. I knew the judgment of God had fallen upon me, but I was hoping that tonight perhaps God would change His mind. He didn't and I only have one thing else to say to you. Please, don't make the same mistake I did." He quickly left the room and I never saw him again, but sometime later I found out he had died. I have never smelled a stench like that since.

The last sense in the Spirit is knowing. This knowledge is given to me without the help of any of the other senses. It is the most difficult of the six to move in, because you have no backup to confirm various knowledge you have suddenly acquired. This last sense is the most refined one in my gifting, and I will share a couple of different examples to better explain what I'm talking about and then give some more when I talk about the Word of Knowledge a little bit later.

BABY I'M THE LUCKY ONE

1. Recently I dealt with a woman I had known years ago as a teenager. She had taken somewhat of a sabbatical as far as God was concerned, and she was recently making her way back. Bad choices in our lives always bring about condemnation from the enemy, and to escape it is easier said than done. She was feeling that same condemnation when I said several things to her about what she was feeling, but this one statement brought tears to her eyes. Her husband was sitting next to her when I told her this, "You feel like your marriage to your husband is similar to the song Amy Grant sings, 'I'm the lucky one.'" It was then that she burst out in tears. After a while, she then composed herself enough to say this, "I just said that same statement to him before we came to church today." Without another word, her expression began to say to me, how did you know? How in the world did you know? I then explained to her, that's just how much God

really did love her and it also confirmed that He was still by her side.

ALLERGIC TO PEPPER

2. Several years ago, we dealt with a woman with horrible allergies. In trying to discern from the Lord what to do with her to get her healing, she went on to say that eating pepper was a death sentence because the allergic reaction would cause so much swelling in her neck area that she would choke to death. I told her that the only way we could find out if in fact God would heal her, after the prayer we needed to confirm it by having her taste some pepper. I asked her if she was willing to do that, and she responded with a resounding yes. I asked her how long it would take for her to negatively react to the pepper and she said pretty much immediately. So we prayed in the name of Jesus, gave her some pepper to eat, and we waited, and waited, and waited. About five minutes or so later there was no swelling, there was no negative reaction to the pepper as well. She was so beside herself, understanding what God had just done, she invited everyone after the service to go celebrate with her at the barbecue restaurant known for its peppery barbecue. So many years after the fact, when we

return to her church, she always comes up to me to greet me and says the same thing with a smile. "I'm still eating pepper with no reaction, PRAISE GOD!"

THE WORD OF KNOWLEDGE

The word of knowledge is a supernatural revelation of natural things from the physical world, both past and present. Usually it is something general, but at times it can become very, very specific because God wants to deal with issues in a person's life that have been hidden from everyone else. When the Word of Knowledge is in the embryonic stage, don't get intimidated by people either lying to you or who out of embarrassment don't want to admit what God has shown to you. Stick to your guns, but if need be, ask God to help you bow out gracefully. Never defend yourself, because the Lord knows how to fix a situation that has gone wrong.

THE FALSE PROPHET IS EXONERATED

Here is an example when I had to not necessarily admit that I was wrong, but because it was a prophecy that had a particular time frame, I had to wait almost an entire year, and I was somewhat vilified until God brought it to pass in an unexpected way. I prophesied over a young lady that by the end of the calendar year the Lord would give her twins. There were several problems in accepting that prophecy in that first of all, she wasn't married, and it didn't look like that would happen anytime soon. The truth of the matter was she didn't have a boyfriend either, so how was all of this going to come to pass? Of course, there are times that God will not allow you to know how He is going to do it, nevertheless our job is to say what God has told us to say and let Him work out the details. For the next few months until the end of the year, I was considered a false prophet. There were quite a few people and churches alike that saw my ministry in a negative light. At the end of the year, I received a phone call from that same young lady, blurting out, "Brother, your prophecy came to pass." I was dumbfounded by her statement and I asked her to please explain. She said, "We found out that my sister who had been jailed was pregnant at the time. Because her sentence was for several years, she would not be able to keep the child and it would have to be put up for adoption. She then asked me if I would be willing to take her child. Of course, I said. But the greatest surprise was this. When she finally gave birth, there was not only one girl born, but like in the prophecy they were twins." When a Word of Knowledge seems to be incomplete, don't fill in the blanks to make yourself look good. God knows what He's doing and our job is to say what has been told us, nothing more and nothing less. Or like my wife says, don't add so much salsa to your tacos!

CAUGHT BEFORE IT WAS TOO LATE

Here is another example of a Word of Knowledge that really built my faith when my gifting was still in the embryo stage. I was preaching in a church that was very demonstrative in its worship. There was a lot of dancing and jumping, running and shouting all throughout the preliminaries. I noticed one particular man who was beside himself in his praises unto God. Out of the corner of my eye, the Lord had me zeroing in on his wife who had stayed in her pew, looking at him with disdain. The Lord then admonished me to go and minister to her. Without a clue as to what I was going to say, I said this to her in her ear: "I know that your boyfriend is waiting for you after the service to take you away and never come back. It would be the biggest mistake of your life, because not only would it ruin your marriage and your family, but even worse it would ruin your relationship with God." Immediately she broke down and wept, sorely repenting of what she had planned to do. She knew that no one could have told me because no one else knew what was going on. For someone from another state to say to her what I did, it had to come from God.

There is one last thing I would like to mention about Words of Knowledge. I know that the next Scripture I will refer to was not written with the Word of Knowledge in mind, nevertheless I believe it fits in what I am about to say.

MESSAGES I DID NOT WANT TO DELIVER

... He who increases knowledge increases sorrow.

(Ecclesiastes 1:18)

Many times, people don't understand the harrowing situations God puts us in to deliver a message that more times than not will bring a negative response. At times in the Old Testament, prophets were beaten, jailed, and sometimes even killed over the messages they had to deliver to those in authority, and yet the Lord sent them anyway because His word needed to be delivered.

Although most of the messages I deliver are positive in nature, there are times I have to say things that I know will cut deep in the heart of those receiving it. I remember having to tell a pastor that one of his young people was going to die, and of course it was hard to swallow because everyone else to that point was believing for a miracle. The young man died shortly after that.

PLAYING HANGMAN

As hard as that was, it didn't even come close to the message God asked me to deliver to a close friend of mine. For years I had so admired his simple childlike faith. It allowed him to ascend very quickly in the kingdom of God. It appeared that things came so easy for him, and the blessings of God followed him wherever he went. After a period of time, things started to go south for him in every area of his life. My admiration for him never stopped me from interceding with God on his behalf, until one day what God revealed to me was utterly horrifying. The Lord rarely ever uses visions to speak to me, but in this case He wanted to play games. In my vision I saw the game of hangman, kind of the old school way of playing Wheel of Fortune.

He set things up this way:

__ __ __ __ ~ __ __ __ __ __ __ __. I was then asked to fill in the blanks. Immediately I figured out the first portion and I quickly dismissed it, because surely he was not dabbling in PORN. I was then instructed by the Lord to bring it to his attention so he could be set free. Why was I placed in such a no-win situation? If I was wrong and accused a man of God wrongfully, what would be the repercussions? But then again, if I was right and did nothing about it, what would happen to his soul? I finally got the guts to call him, stumbling and fumbling over my words until I asked him if he wanted to play a game of hangman. Amused by my request, he said all right. When I told him to take out a paper and draw the lines in the way that I arranged them above, there was silence on the other side of the line. He immediately figured out the puzzle and then shocked me by admitting it was true. We got him help to deal with this addiction, and now he is a completely different person.

When God decides to use you to deliver a message to someone, very much like a policeman on twenty-four-hour watch, we must put aside the consequences and do what is right. If you can approach God with that kind of attitude, then He will trust you with secrets you will have to take out of darkness into His marvelous light, so that those stuck in their sin can be brought out, forgiven, and given a new lease on life.

YOU CAN'T ALWAYS SAY WHAT YOU KNOW

One last word of caution regarding the use of the Word of Knowledge. Years ago, I was told by a man of God something that goes against the grain of how we use the Word of Knowledge in the world today. He said that 80 percent of revelation should never be said in public. Going back to the Scripture in Ecclesiastes 1:18, one must consider: Why would knowledge cause so much sorrow? The answer to that question is simple in that just because something is brought to your attention and knowledge doesn't necessarily mean it should be said in public. Any time you have to sit on revelation, there is always this temptation to say what you know. A mature Christian knows how to button the lip and therefore has to endure sorrows that are not privy to everyone else, because God can trust you to keep that secret. I have had to make wholesale changes in my thinking, recognizing that people lie to me all the time. What is even worse is when those lies come from the mouths of pastors themselves. Not responding to those lies is one of the most difficult things I have had to endure, but nevertheless it's part of the job and must be put up with.

Finally, consider the challenge Jesus faced when as a child He knew He was born to ultimately become the long-awaited Messiah who would take away the sins of the world. It appeared that He almost blew His cover as a twelve-year-old when He stayed back in Jerusalem during Passover to "be about his Father's business." Can you imagine the pressure He must have felt when a childhood friend suddenly died, and although He had the power to resurrect him from the dead, because it was not yet time, He had to back away? That waiting period dragged on for thirty long years.

THE DISCERNING OF SPIRITS

The discerning of spirits by definition is: a supernatural revelation of the spirit world. In dealing with the spirit world, one must know what he is dealing with, whether it be the Spirit of God, man's spirit, or Satan. Many people erroneously take it for granted that any kind of negative commotion in our lives is initiated by Satan. Sad to say, many negative problems surface from our flesh and not Satan. I heard this testimony years ago from Pastor Billy Cole that I would like to share. While in the missionary field, I believe it was in Thailand, a particular woman was disrupting the service by showing signs of being demon possessed. She was able to slither on the floor like a snake and had unnaturally strong strength. When Brother Cole was able to discern the situation, it was brought to his attention that all the commotion was not spirit induced. Rather, she was a woman who needed a lot of attention, so she reacted in ways that she could be noticed. As soon as Brother Cole instructed the ushers to take her outside, she immediately ceased her antics and was dealt with accordingly.

On the other hand, there are two friends of mine who are very sensitive to the spirit world, yet they are polar opposites in that Martin's experiences with spirits came from the diabolical side. Missti's experience with the spirit world has to deal with angels. When Martin was first converted and experienced Pentecost for the first time after receiving the Holy Ghost, he began to freak out at what he was seeing, because it was very much like what his experience was before he came to the Lord. After one of these episodes, he spoke to the pastor utterly confused. He wanted to know why after being saved and Spirit-filled, he was still able to see demons raising havoc amongst various members of the church. Somewhat bewildered by this, because he had never heard anything like this before, his pastor instructed him that at the next service, if and when he saw those demons again, to call him so he could pray for those who were being bothered by those spirits. Missti, on the other hand, has had angels following her from the time she was between five or seven years old, if I'm not mistaken. Because she was prostituted as a child (not her choice) and then kicked out of the church, God would send angels to her to teach the oracles of God. She sees angels all the time and subsequently directs them to certain people who are in trouble, to allow them to minister through the Spirit of God so they can be blessed.

THE YOUNG LADY WITH LILAC MAKEUP

Finally, I would like to share one of the experiences I have had dealing with the spirit world. Years ago, I was invited to a particular church that in the past I thoroughly enjoyed ministering in. The pastor and his family were very gracious and kind to me, and their daughters were pretty much the same age as my oldest son, Timothy. In getting to know the girls, I liked what I saw in that they were unreservedly dedicated to the things of the Lord. That being said, I was in utter shock when I saw the oldest daughter walk in really late to service and her outer appearance wasn't anything like the young lady I had known in the past. Her clothing was more snug than usual, and to my surprise she was all made up (our modesty beliefs discourage makeup). When I made the altar call, she did come, but again laying hands on her, I noticed the nail polish that matched her makeup and lipstick she was wearing as well. When service was over, I made it a point to greet her, but to my surprise, there was no makeup, there was no lipstick, and there was no nail polish on her hands. The Lord then spoke to me and said this, "She is living a double life, unbeknownst to her parents." I was saddened by the fact that she had gone away from our Pentecostal ways, but what was even sadder is this: I never saw her again.

Demonic spirits have the ability to attack in various ways and different levels. Satan is highly organized and will use any method necessary to keep children of God away from their destiny. Because my experience in this area is so limited, I decided to recruit a couple of folks whose expertise will better explain the "Discerning of Spirits."

APOSTOLIC DEMONOLOGY

(DAVID & MISSTI JONES)

For we wrestle not against flesh and blood, but against principalities, against powers, against the rulers of the darkness of this world, against spiritual wickedness in high places.

Ephesians 6:12 (KJV)

Lest Satan should get an advantage of us: for we are not ignorant of his devices.

2 Corinthians 2:11 (KJV)

(For the weapons of our warfare are not carnal, but mighty through God to the pulling down of strong holds;)

2 Corinthians 10:4 (KJV)

Submit yourselves therefore to God. Resist the devil, and he will flee from you.

James 4:7

My name is Sis. Missti L. Jones. I am the wife of Apostolic Demonologist, Rev. David G. Jones, and I am what 1 Corinthians 12:10 calls a "Spirit Discerner." God chose to give me that gift of the Spirit when I was five years old, a few months after I was filled with the Holy Ghost. I started to "see" both demons and angels by the time I was seven years old, and my pastor would use my gift to help him deal with demonically possessed people who would come into our church for help.

Both my husband and I are also veterans of the US Armed Forces (My husband was in the US Air Force, and I was in the US Army). Our extensive military experience and combat training walk hand-in-hand in my husband's ministry. He is an apostolic evangelist whose specialty is spiritual warfare and demonology. He also has vital knowledge of the allies God has given us on the field of spiritual battle: Angels (there are many different classes of angels, and each class has their own set of specific "battle" skills for the children of God to use. It cuts our duration of trials or spiritual battles in half). I'm just going to be talking about demons, the different stages of a demonic attack on a person, place, or thing, how to identify what stage of demonic attack you or your church might be under, and how to defeat each stage. I'll also share a few of the demonic cases my husband and I have dealt with. Think of my husband as King David, and I am his "seer," Gad, who can physically see the spiritual world in real time, and be the "eyes" for not only my husband and his ministry, but other ministers who have contacted me for help when going through spiritual battles, but satan and his imps were blocking their spiritual sight and they needed a "Gad" to help see through the smoke grenades detonated by our enemy the devil.

First things first: what does "Demonology" mean?

Demonology is the study of demons. You might think there was something more spooky or glorious about it, but you would be wrong. It's very simple. An apostolic demonologist, like my husband, is an Acts 2:38 doctrine preaching, "*Ye shall receive power from on high*" believing, satan will know your name like Jesus and Paul, aisle running, filled with the Holy Ghost, baptized in Jesus' name, anointed child of God who has familiarized themselves with their weapons of spiritual warfare so much, it has "melted" onto their hand, like the mighty men of valor who fought alongside King David, and can use it like Hebrews 4:12 to the "*dividing asunder*" of any demonic entity that may come! Makes me want to run aisles just thinking about it, KNOWING that THAT little creature from the pits of hell MUST BOW before the name above all names: Jesus Christ, and he and his legions of demons SHALL FLEE from us if we only RESIST him! Glory!

As a Veteran of the US Army, one of the best tips I can give any of you reading this book is this: KNOW YOUR ENEMY!

You can't defeat an enemy you're totally ignorant or naive about! You will just go into battle underestimating the enemy, and just like the Seven Sons of Sceva (Acts 19:14-17), you will leave the spiritual battle field running in defeat at best, or physically, mentally, emotionally, or God forbid, spiritually injured, and make matters worse than when you started. Remember: satan and his crew of misfits have been doing this kind of thing since before Adam and Eve. DO NOT UNDERESTIMATE HIM! It is NOT YOU who can defeat him and his imps! It's ONLY through the authority in the name of Jesus Christ that you will defeat him! Never forget that! When we get too big for our britches, and we start making ourselves a "god" like King Saul did, bad things can and will happen. Just like a real soldier, marine, sailor, or airman, you MUST keep your head clear and focus on the task at hand! Why? Because satan and his crew will use magic, parlor tricks, fear, doubt, blackmail, shame, guilt, disease; literally everything he used against Job...EXPECT IT! Learn to "see" it for what it is! Adapt! Never let him control your mind, emotions, or diminish your faith in the Word of God: your sword!

For God hath not given us the spirit of fear; but of power, and of love, and of a sound mind.

(2 Timothy 1:7).

So, let's get to know the basics of our enemy: the devil.

Demonic attacks, no matter what stage, usually occurs during what is known as the "Witching Hour," between 9 pm, and 3 am. Pastors, don't be shocked if your phones ring off the hook for spiritual issues during these hours. It's not a matter of IF it will happen, it's a matter of WHEN it will happen! Expect it, and plan accordingly. During this time is when most people will feel attacked in their homes, cars, boats, planes, or at work, and families can often find themselves fighting for no reason during these hours.

Satan can possess three known earthly things:

1. Things (1 Samuel 5:1-5)
2. Places (Genesis 18 and 19)
3. People/Animals (Mark 5:1-15)

There are stages of possession. It is vital that you know what stage you are dealing with, because that will dictate how you need to deal with that specific enemy on that specific spiritual battlefield (Matthew 17:14-21). If you can catch satan and his little demonic critters as they are creeping into a person, place, or thing at the very beginning, you can spiritually flick it like a bug and be done with them easily. However, if a person comes to you and the church, and they've allowed satan to move in with all his demonic little knick-knacks, friends, and set up shop, well now things will get spiritually sporty, and you are going to have to behave like the "Elite Special Forces" of the Apostolic church! You are going to have to rely on your "training." You're going to have to rely on the Word of God. And you are going to have to sacrifice your flesh by fasting and praying for at least three days, if not more (my husband and I have had to pray and fast for seven days before on a case) to get rid of this spiritual lice, because you aren't going to be dealing with regular Joey Bag-O-Doughnuts Demons. You will be dealing with something much stronger. Something like a Legion, or even satan himself! DO NOT BE UNPREPARED! A person(s)' life may depend upon how "spiritually strong" you have kept yourself for "Such A Time As This." Not to mention, you could get you and your brothers and sisters in Christ who are there helping you hurt physically and/or spiritually if you are not right with God, or where you need to be spiritually for this kind of spiritual warfare. Satan plays for keeps. Never forget that! He is a sly little creature, just waiting for you to make a mistake...so try your best not to. You need to keep "spiritually fit," just like soldiers stay "physically fit" to succeed on the field of spiritual battle. How do you do that? By "working out" spiritually: praying, fasting, reading the Word of God (push-ups, sit-ups, two-mile run, metaphorically speaking).

THE FIVE STAGES OF DEMONIC POSSESSION

There are five basic stages of demonic possession:

Depression/Attachment
Infestation
Oppression
Possession
Perfect Possession

Depression/Attachment:

If you can flank satan and his demons at the first stage, Depression/Attachment, and identify that battle maneuver, then a simple laying on of hands at the altar, literally by anyone with a mustard seed of faith, can help the person suffering by rebuking that demonic attack, and push it back to the pits of hell where it belongs. Too easy! One of the demonic depression cases my husband and I were asked to pray for was for a teenage girl who was attacked with depression. She couldn't explain why she felt depressed, only that she was. Keep in mind that teenagers and elderly (especially if they are entering puberty, menopause, or they just suffered a loss of a spouse or have to be admitted to a nursing home) suffer the most with this specific kind of demonic attack. Women who just gave birth, with their hormones all out of whack, also tend to be easy targets due to sleep deprivation, and loss of strength physically and spiritually due to the birthing process (or miscarriage). Keep a close spiritual eye on these people in church. Satan loves to attack the vulnerable, because he is a big coward! He doesn't like to fight someone he knows is spiritually strong, though make no mistake, if he can take down a "mighty man/woman of valor" he will! Never go into battle with your eyes closed.

Everyone has experienced a demonic attachment at one time or another. You can get a demonic attachment simply by going into an antique or secondhand store and touching items in the store. You have no clue who owned those items, or what they were used for. They could have been used for all kinds of demonic worship. It's never a bad idea to pray over yourself, or items you buy, before bringing these things into your home. Prayer NEVER hurts!

Infestation:
This is the second stage. It's a little more creepy if you've never seen or experienced it. This usually affects places more than anything else. Such as: homes, cars, ships, planes, businesses, forests,

parks, and other buildings. Depending on how long satan and his creepy band of brothers have decided to take a vacation in that particular place for the season, getting rid of these spiritual rodents shouldn't be too hard for you. Even children can help cast these critters out, with the proper training on how to do it, and I am a firm believer in "training a child up in the ways of the Lord." What if your kid is alone, and this infestation happens? Do you train them to spiritually defend themselves like Daniel, Meshach, Shadrach, and Abednego had been clearly trained to do? Or do you leave them for the enemy to exploit, and now you have bigger issues, because satan has just attached to your kids, depression sets in, and BOOM! You have a full-blown possession on your hands? Nope! I'll stick with training the kids to fight satan, thank you very much! I can ALWAYS use a good "Daniel" on my team! Praise God!

Not everyone is a Spirit Discerner or has one available to "see" which demons are attacking, or where they are hiding. Keep in mind, ALL DEMONS TRAVEL IN THREES: Demon of Lies, Demon of Fear, and then the third demon will be the main demon controlling the other two, like a military "Team Leader," and dictating how the enemy is fighting on the spiritual field of battle. There could be more, but you know right out of the gate you are dealing with AT LEAST three!

The Demon of Fear will cause things like a feeling of being watched, but you are completely alone in your car, room, or building. It will start throwing darts at your mind telling you that you are weak, or satan is going to kill you or your family. It will cause you to think people you love hate you, your church is ashamed of you because of your past or are gossiping about you, and you aren't good enough for God to love or use you. It can cause a room to rain, temperature fluctuations, the animals in your house to start acting strange, things to start flying across the room, but you can't "see" anyone who tossed it, scratch you, slap you, throw you, levitate you, and make you feel sick to your stomach, especially if you are filled with the Holy Ghost and baptized in Jesus' name. Don't be surprised if you, or people in the room/building, vomit green or red goo (bile). And the vomit won't be "natural." It will shoot out to an ungodly three feet or more, or like what happened to our son, vomit that goes up to the ceiling, instead of on the floor.

The Demon of Lies will block your spiritual sight at this stage, and make you THINK that everything is okay, but the Holy Ghost (gut feeling) will insist that little spook is still hiding! This demon is an EXPERT hide-and-seek player! Don't be fooled! With the other demon(s), you will have to wait until you get to the infestation to determine what it is.

What you need to do at this stage is follow the perfect example God gave to Moses to anoint homes. The same technique is used for cars, boats, planes, and other buildings. Parks or forests are a little different, and I'll explain that at the end of this section. My husband and I use oil in place of lamb's blood, because Jesus was the perfect Lamb who shed His blood to heal all things. We have used water and salt before, and they work, but our own personal preference is olive oil. We pray over it, and ask God to bless it, and let it represent His blood shed on the cross and remind Him of His promise to us: By His stripes, we are healed. Before we start casting out demons, we anoint ALL the people in the home who do not have the Holy Ghost, all children, also all animals. Remember: Legion leaped into pigs, then caused them to jump off a cliff and kill themselves. We have witnessed this happen before.

A church couple who are friends of ours forgot to pray over their dog before they started praying over their home and left their little beagle on a leash tied up on their front porch. While praying in the house, a demon leaped into the dog, the dog jumped off the porch, and hung itself. PRAY OVER YOUR ANIMALS! The last thing you need is to open a demonic door of depression, especially if you have kids, and mourn over a lost pet because you forgot to take a few seconds to pray over your furry family. We then anoint ALL doorposts (top and both sides) to include closets and cabinets, mirrors (used as a portal for demons to travel, which are why witches use them to this day for scrying), and over all beds so satan can penetrate your dreams and give people nightmares while they are sleeping. If dealing with cars, boats, or planes, we also anoint the engines so satan can't manipulate the electrical systems to cause a crash or demonic foolery. For parks and forests, pray over a piece of cloth after you anoint it with oil, and bury it on the property. This will heal the land and give satan his eviction notice.

There will also be signs that you are dealing with an infestation. A home is in disarray, because satan loves chaos. Or, you could have a tidy home, but a foul smell of rotting meat, or something dead. You might hear something scratching on the walls, similar to rats or raccoons scratching or knocking. The knocking will come in threes: Boom! Boom! Boom! Poltergeist (German for: Angry Ghost) is a scientifically proven spiritual phenomenon that also occurs at this stage. You can leave a room perfectly tidy and normal for a few moments, and come back in, and the furniture is stacked to deny gravity, all the dresser or cabinet doors/drawers are open, and stuff is everywhere, yet no one "did it." This is all the Demon of Fear trying to make you open a door for the next stage...

Oppression:

During this third stage, at least one person in the home, usually the most vulnerable or the strongest (because hey, if satan can take out the "general," the privates are easy pickings!) will come under direct spiritual attack. If you are dealing with teenagers: WATCH FOR SIGNS OF CUTTING or SELF-MUTILATION (1 Kings 18:28). If they are cutting themselves, then you know you are dealing with a "Principality" named Baal, and you can start your Holy Ghost "rebuking" attack on him! The target of satan/demonic attack will tell you that they are hearing voices telling them to hurt themselves, co-workers, school mates, church folks, strangers, animals, and if they don't comply, the voice(s) claim that it will kill someone they love in retaliation for not doing as commanded. At this point, you MUST determine if the victim of this demonic oppression attack is suffering from a medical or mental illness. You don't want to go in Apostolic Hero-cape and all, and come to find out the person is on some kind of mind-altering medication, illegal street drug, alcohol, just came out of an medical operation recently, or is being treated for some kind of mental health issues. Once all that has been eliminated, then you are dealing with something spiritual and not physical. I've lost count with how many teenagers my husband and I have dealt with at this stage of oppression in the church who had started cutting themselves. This is a plague in our churches, folks! Don't be fooled! All you must do at this stage is anoint the victim and pray over them exactly the way you would for anyone who would call upon the elders of the church for prayer to be healed. You might have to pray a few times, because satan will try to come back and tempt the victim to cut, self-mutilate, or become oppressed again. There is no shame in it. Most of the time, it's not the victim's fault (they weren't playing with Ouija boards or doing a séance). Just pray again until they are spiritually free from the attack. It's always best to pray for these victims on holy ground (in church). But, you might not have that kind of time or opportunity, depending on the situation. We can't always pick where satan chooses to fight us.

The fourth, and most dangerous stage for the victim (now the "host"), you, your family, and the entire church, will be:

Possession:

Satan and demons can possess people, animals, and objects (dolls, pictures, mirrors, etc.). When dealing with a possessed object, you need to anoint it, pray a "binding" prayer over it (I bind you in the name and blood of Jesus Christ), and then you want to dispose of it properly. My husband and I remove it from the victim's home and keep it locked up. That way no one else will get hold of it and "loosen" it back onto someone or themselves. The best thing to do is bury it with a prayer cloth. I don't recommend burning it. Some of these items are infested with so much evil that they won't burn, or you could feel like you are burning when the item is burning, especially if you aren't spiritually strong enough to deal with whatever it is. It doesn't mean you can't. But if you are dealing with something like a Ouija board, I'd advise against burning it. Bind it and bury it in a place no one will find it, to include animals. Also, if you have hit this stage, and you choose to help the host because they've asked for help (which is VITAL, due to the free will God gave us all), NEVER STOP CASTING OUT DEMONS UNTIL THE PERSON IS TOTALLY FREE AND PRAY THEM THROUGH TO THE HOLY GHOST! You NEVER want to leave the possessed host empty after spending all that time casting demons out of them! Those demons will just go get seven more...EACH...and bring them back to re-possess that person, and now you've done more harm than good! Don't start if you are not going to finish! (Matthew 12:45, Luke 11:26)

If you are dealing with a possessed animal, anoint it with oil, rebuke the demons out of it, and ask God to loosen peace and comfort to the animal to keep it safe, like He cares for the sparrows in the sky. Even a hedge of protection was put over Job's animals. It wasn't until God removed it due to satan pouting about not being able to attack Job, that God did, and the animals were killed. PRAYER NEVER HURTS!

If you are dealing with human possession, hold onto your seat because it's going to get sporty! You will want to keep a "possession kit" that contains garbage bags, paper towels, gloves, oil, and your Bible in it. As demons come out of a human host, the host tends to vomit, and the paper towels will help clean that up, and you can toss it into the trash bags, as you keep rebuking demons. Jesus never put His hands on someone who was possessed, but in Acts we see that the disciples "laid hands" on them and cast them out. However, more times than not, they simply rebuked the demons without touching the host, and the demons fled.

Why is that important?
Because we know that demons can leap from one host to another. It's best to not allow them to leap onto you. Have you ever tried to fight with someone hanging off of you? Yeah. Not a good idea! This is also where the Demon of Lies comes

into play the most. It will say things like, "Thank you, pastor! It's all gone! No more! You can stop now!" yet you can still feel the thickness in the air, the face and/or body of the host is still contorted, and the host can't seem to say the name of Jesus at all. They will still have a "hissing" sound when they speak and may even slither. Don't believe that little liar! Rebuke it in Jesus' name and keep fighting! Try the spirit! If the person finally starts praying, and able to say, "I love You, Jesus!" CONGRATS! You have left the possession stage and are entering into the filling of the Holy Ghost stage! Keep going until the victim is filled with the Holy Ghost and is turned into a survivor!

The very first demonic possession case I was on, my pastor, district Presbyter, and a handful of other elder brothers in the church (plus my pastor's wife) had a young man sitting at the altar. I was seven years old, and I could see these hideous creatures speaking into the ear of the man, while flying in and out of his body. It was the first time I ever saw a demon. I closed my eyes real tight, as my pastor's wife had me sit down several pews back from the men. She hugged me tight, and the Presbyter, who knew about my gift said, "Sissy, tell me what you see." I shook my head 'no' and began to cry because I was so scared. The demons were cussing and saying all kinds of foul things about the men of the church trying to cast them out, and all I wanted to do was go home! I didn't want to see or hear any of it!

My Presbyter said, "Sissy, this will go a lot faster if you can tell me what the demons are saying. Can you tell me their names?"

I said, "Pastor, they are cussing and saying bad things! I'll sin if I tell you what they are saying," and began to bawl. The demons manipulated my emotions to make me feel I would be a dirty rotten sinner if I helped the elders of the church cast these demons out of this host.

My pastor's wife hugged me tight, and whispered gently in my ear, "If you like, you can repent later. But can you tell Pastor the names at least? It will make this young man feel much better."

I then began to list off the names of the demons in the young man. In the end, there were fourteen demons possessing that man. During the deliverance, I was levitated off the pew, which really scared me. I began to cry harder. My pastor told me to "focus" and that "For God hath not given you the spirit of fear, but of power, and of love, and of a sound mind." Because I trusted my pastor so much (he was like a grandpa to me), I opened my eyes, and that was when I saw my first angel: my guardian angel who is with me all day long, and I see all the time now. He was flying beside me. Once I focused on a godly thing, I began to laugh, because at seven years old, I thought I was flying with the angels. That was when the demons stopped levitating me and dropped me. My angel caught me and set me down gently back on the pew, then stood in front of me with his sword drawn. The Holy Ghost was so powerful at that point, I was no longer scared anymore. They didn't stop fighting, until the young man started speaking in tongues as God filled him with the Holy Ghost. I watched as archangels dragged the demons out of the host by the hair of their heads, and right through the wall outside every time the brethren cast one out. It was awesome to witness! That young man is now an elderly man, married, with several children, and living for God still today. NEVER GIVE UP! This is also the one state where you might have to embrace the "sacrifice" and pray and fast for a few days before you start fighting satan for the soul of this person. It depends on what the main demon is, how long it has been allowed to fester in its host, and how many might be with it.

Perfect Possession:

The final stage, and one that is literally out of your control, is Perfect Possession. My husband and I have dealt with this one time in our lives. This is where the human host WANTS to be possessed. They enjoy the false sense of power and control satan makes them feel. We see this with Jezebel in the Bible. She was a worshiper of Baal and loved being a servant of her demon. Due to free will that all humans are given, there is nothing you can do at this stage.

A few years ago, our pastor asked us to go and look into the possible possession of a home. An elderly woman had called the church for help, because she felt her house was haunted, and claimed to want help. As soon as we pulled up to the property, I saw a demon sitting on her porch, smiling at us. I touched my husband, who had gathered his "possession kit" and was getting ready to walk onto the property. I also saw our two guardian angels draw their swords, which is very rare for them to do. Usually I only see archangels, or the Destroyer angel do that. My angel then told me, "This is a trick!" and I relayed the message to my husband. I advised that we pray a prayer of protection upon us outside instead of inside the home, and asked the angels to also pray with us, like angels had done with Samson's parents, and with Gideon. Once we felt the Holy Ghost engulf us, we entered the home.

The woman's face had this evil smile on it, as she welcomed us into her home. We were immediately hit with a foul rotting meat smell. Flies and maggots had infested the home even though it was tidy, and I saw a mirror with different colored used candles lying on the coffee table. I could smell sulfur, and the wicks were smoldering still, as if she just blew them out. She had been scrying as we pulled up in our car!

My husband can't see demons or angels like me, but he can spiritually feel when things are "off." We went room to room, as the smell of death followed us. She kept trying to reach out and touch my husband's back when he wasn't looking but couldn't seem to do it. It was like an invisible shield had engulfed him, and each time she tried, she grabbed her hand back as if she was being burned. She then scooted off to a couch in her front room where the mirror and candles were, and as my husband walked into one of the rooms to investigate, I kept my eye on the old woman. She started rocking back and forth, clutching her hands together. I then saw a big black shadow mass seep out of her, and then sucked back into her. I walked cautiously into the room, a good distance away from her, and asked her if she was all right, knowing the answer already: she wasn't.

She said, "There are times I black out, and when I wake up, I don't know where I am, or how I got there. I woke up in the park before, naked. But I feel so strong! I'm more powerful than you and your God!"

She then started speaking German (I know because I was stationed in Hanau, Germany, when I was in the US Army), and her face contorted. She leaped at me, and stretched out her arms to touch me, but it was like her arms became too short to reach all of a sudden.

Because all I saw was a big black mass, I couldn't identify the demon. "By the authority and power of the Name of Jesus Christ, what is your name demon!" I demanded.

By this time, my husband came running into the room, and the woman began to cackle. My husband took out his oil, and as soon as he put a dab on her forehead, her entire body contorted into an ungodly shape, her hands turned into claws, and her feet went into the shape of hooves, though they still looked like human feet.

"Don't do this! I don't want them to go! They are my friends!" she screamed.

My husband then ordered the demon to allow the old woman to speak in Jesus' name. The old woman's body went limp on the couch, her face was no longer smiling weird or contorted, and she was panting heavily as sweat ran down her face. My husband then began to speak to the human soul of this elderly woman. "Do you want the demons gone? Do you want to be delivered of this?"

"No," she answered. "It took me so long to get them to come to me. Without them I am weak. They are my friends. They give me strength and power. If you take them from me, I will be lost, and empty. If I knew you both could get rid of my friends, I wouldn't have called."

"You wanted to get a spiritual trophy for your demon, didn't you?" I asked her. "You thought you could just trick a child of the Most High God to come to your home, and ensnare them into a trap, and sacrifice them to your demon! Well, you chose the wrong people to do that to! Now I am going to ask for God to deal with you the same way He dealt with Nebuchadnezzar! You will have the same fate as him for trying to hurt children of the Great I Am!"

At that moment we knew she had chosen this life, she wanted it, and thought we were game for her to prey on. That was her mistake! My husband and I left, and before the week was out, she was admitted to a mental hospital, where even the Catholic priest wouldn't go into her room to deal with her. She had lost her mind just like I told her she would.

Know the enemy. Familiarize yourself with the weapons God gave you. They should be an extension of your body, like a weapon is to a soldier. Trust God. Don't be afraid to ask God to send angels to help you. Never let fear control your emotions or things you know to be true in God's Word. Have faith in God. No weapon formed against you shall prosper. Amen.

THE WORD OF WISDOM

This is probably one of the easiest gifts of the Spirit to define because it is nothing more than knowing how to apply or what to do in a given situation when a Word of Knowledge is given. This particular gift kicks tradition to the curb and is highly criticized by most people who don't understand how God speaks to us. It will many times go against the status quo, and even more puzzling is when there are no biblical examples to confirm the instructions we are receiving from God. The Word of Wisdom is the best example of a rhema revelation and usually will startle if not bewilder those who have never heard anything like that. Many come to the conclusion that what is being uttered is nothing more than nonsense or a type of grandstanding to make the person delivering the message greater than what they are.

But God has chosen the foolish things of the world to put to shame the wise, and God has chosen the weak things of the world to put to shame the things which are mighty.

(1 Corinthians 1:27)

Here are some biblical examples that explain how a Word of Wisdom was applied. Notice that for every different circumstance there was a different action taken to receive an answer. Every action, as different as they were, all had one thing in common. For the person in need to receive their petition, it had to include a step of faith.

EXAMPLES OF A WORD OF WISDOM

Naaman, a man of authority stricken with leprosy, was asked to go bathe in the Jordan River, dipping himself seven times to receive his healing. When finally convinced to do so, there was no trace of leprosy at all. (2 Kings 5:1-14)

Jesus sent a blind man with mud pasted on his eyes to the pool of Siloam, which was not the pool for healing. Without instructions how to get there, without any help, this blind man had to navigate the journey by himself to the pool Jesus was sending him to. Once there, he washed and was healed. (John 9:1-7)

One day on the Sabbath, Jesus encountered a man with a withered hand. He simply said, "Stretch out your hand." He was immediately healed. (Matthew 12:13)

Peter encountered a man who was lame since birth at the gate of the temple and instructed him to simply "get up and walk." Peter then took him by the hand, and by faith he not only got up but walk for the first time in his entire life. (Acts 3:1-8)

To pay the taxes that were owed, the Lord sent Peter fishing at the wrong time of the day, with these instructions: When you catch your first fish, open its mouth and you will find the money you need to pay the taxes. (Matthew 17:27)

When some lepers cried out for healing, Jesus instructed them to show themselves to the priests, and as they went they were healed. Jesus didn't even pray for them, their obedience brought their healing. (Luke 17:12-14)

When the friends of a lame man cut open the roof of the building Jesus was speaking in, it was enough for the Lord to heal their friend. (Mark 2:1-12)

THE GIFT OF FAITH

The gift of faith is not the measure of faith you and I receive at the time of salvation. The gift of faith is in reality God's faith. It is released when the Lord would like to perform an extraordinary miracle through man that normally cannot be done.

When I first started working in the gifts of the Spirit, I felt so inadequate because I was convinced that my ability to be successful in this ministry would be found lacking. It did nothing for my confidence to be put in situations where I felt the situation was way above my pay grade. Nevertheless, it was part of my training to get to where I am today.

A GREAT LESSON LEARNED IN MEXICO

One such lesson that has had such a profound effect on me was one learned on one of my first trips to Mexico. It was bad enough I didn't speak the language fluently, yet I still got an invitation from a man of God I really did not know well. On one of the nights, I found myself so intimidated I backed away from the assignment that was given to me that day. There was a young lady handicapped from birth who wanted to be healed. She and her mama were visiting the church and heard that the God of its members could perform miracles. Sad to say, I ignored her, hoping she would not return the next night. Utterly convicted by my lack of faith, I just did not believe I had enough faith to help her secure her healing. When the Lord gave me another opportunity the next day, I almost blew that assignment as well. The Lord told me to step out of the moment so we could talk. I then confessed to Him that I was both intimidated by the assignment and scared that I would not be successful. He reminded me that that was certainly the case in every new assignment He had given me in the past. Success would come when I was willing to take a step of faith. In His ultimate wisdom, He understood my faith would not do the trick, so He mercifully filled me with a gift of faith. With God's faith nestled in my bosom, I took a step forward and an anointing fell upon me like I had never experienced before. There was this newfound energy and confidence unknown to me in the past, yet it was the force that allowed me to be in God's perfect will. When I prayed for her the first time, she took a few steps without the help of the apparatus she used pretty much all her life but got tired quickly and I allowed her to sit down. When it came time to pick up the final offering before dismissal, something incredible happened. After that prayer, her initial faith grew to the point that when she made her way to the altar to deposit the little bit of money her mama had, her faith turned into God's faith. As if being shot out of a cannon, she began to run around the church, rejoicing because of the healing she had received.

There will be times in our lives that extraordinary situations will call for extraordinary faith. It will be in these times that the gift of faith will take over, bringing us to a place of victory that could not have happened without God's faith.

THE GIFTS OF HEALING

The Gifts of Healings are not as readily accepted as the Working of Miracles because they are not instantaneous. I believe if we were to always have our druthers, miracles would always trump healing. Nevertheless, God has chosen this vehicle to also be used to bring relief to our sickened bodies. That being said, by definition the gifts of healings are a gradual and progressive restoration of the human body. We must always remember that healing is gradual and the working of miracles is instantaneous.

MORE THAN ONE GIFT

One of the more important lessons I had to learn about the Gifts of Healings was the fact that there was more than one gift. Each and every disease and illness has a gift of healing attached to it, and must have the opportunity to grow to perfection. Initially, you labor through a trial and error period until you have dominion over that disease. The process is repeated constantly, ever stretching your faith to continue growing in your service to Him. At this moment in my ministry, any time I have to deal with anyone suffering with the disease of fibromyalgia, they will heal about each 99 percent of the time. If and when I have to deal with this particular disease, the thought does not even cross my mind that they will not go without their healing.

AN IMPORTANT WORD OF ADVICE

The best word of advice I can give anyone who is interested in starting a ministry of healing is to never begin that ministry in a regular church service. I say that because between unbelief and jealousy running rampant in many of our congregations, the newbie trying to hone his craft in a healing ministry will be put under the microscope and not be allowed to make errors like all of us do when we are doing something new. My best advice would be the same I received when I got started. The man of God said to go to the nearest Walmart and start asking God to show you who needed prayer. You needn't worry about the workers there because they are always hiding anyway when anyone needs help, so why should they stop you from doing God's will?

AN EXPERIENCE AT WALMART

I remember a situation arose at the Walmart in our city that I would like to share. I had just been fitted for a new ankle brace to help me with a drop step that I was suffering from. Because the brace was somewhat bulky and uncomfortable, it was constantly in need of adjustment. When I got there, I found a bench to sit on to make that adjustment, and a man on the other side of the room noticed my brace. He too was handicapped from a stroke he had suffered, leaving him with horrible back pains and walking with a limp. He noticed me before I noticed him and came over and struck up a conversation. Immediately the Word of Knowledge kicked in after I had mentioned that God uses me in a healing ministry. I then told him where in his body the pain was causing the most discomfort. With utter amazement, he admitted it to be true and allowed me to pray for him. The Lord instantaneously took away his pain and he was in awe because he had never seen God perform a miracle before in his life, or in anyone else's life for that matter.

THE WORKING OF MIRACLES

The Working of Miracles is the instantaneous and immediate work of God that applies to all things. This could also include the elements and or the forces of nature.

PRAYING FOR RAIN

Back in the 80s when I was supervising a Christian school, I was trying to instill in our students the importance of prayer and faith. I know that it is easy for us to admit that we do pray, and when needed we can extend our faith, but then again when trying situations arise we are clueless as to how we are going to get out of the mess we find ourselves in.

One gloomy day where the kids were forced to stay inside because of the rain, one of the kids challenged me to pray and make the rain stop. Of course, no one in the classroom believed that was possible, and to tell you the truth I really wasn't too sure myself. But I took a step of faith, and with hands raised I commanded the rain to stop. I was not really expecting anything to happen, but I was not going to tell them that. At that point a great commotion broke out, because immediately the rain stopped. The oohs and ahs did not compare to the looks I got, as if they were saying, "Did he really do what I think he did, stopping the rain?" It was a great object lesson for them and a great faith builder for me.

SHRINK THE TUMORS

The next testimony I would like to share regarding the Working of Miracles happened at a time I was getting my feet wet in ministering in the miraculous, back in the 90s. I received a phone call from a good friend of mine whose wife had suffered a stroke. The doctors had explained to him that the tumors they found in her head were growing very aggressively. If the tumors continued to grow at that rate, they were not sure if they could eventually help her. After getting off the phone, I immediately received specific instructions from the Lord. He was asking me to go on an extended time of prayer and fasting (twenty-one days, water only). I remember starting three different times, the first two ending in failure. For whatever reasons, I just could not get into the flow of this period of sacrifice and it was really eating me up. But the third time was different. So much so that He made a strange request. He said that while I was in prayer during this time, for thirty minutes I was to extend both arms in front of me, opening and closing my hands, repeating, "Shrink the tumors in Jesus' name." In those days, our church doors used to open at 4 AM for morning prayer, and I made sure I was there at 4 AM because I did not want very many people watching me do something that I really was uncomfortable with. Days and even a couple of weeks went by, and I was not feeling anything of God at all, much less feel confident that what I was doing in prayer was really making a difference. The end of those twenty-one days of fasting could not come soon enough, but a couple of days after, I received a phone call from my friend regarding the latest test results. He said that the x-rays were showing that the tumors were shrinking and almost completely gone. When I heard him say the word "shrinking," I almost broke out in my happy dance. Those of you who know me know that I do not have a happy dance, but I was extremely happy. Why all the theatrics? Couldn't God have just taken over the situation and shrunk the tumors without my help? Undoubtedly so, but we cannot avoid the declaration God has given us through His Word that says:

For we are laborers together with God...

(1 Corinthians 3:9)

There has to be a connection between heaven and earth so that those who do not know Him can see just how great and mighty is the God we serve.

The last example I would like to leave of the Working of Miracles is one that is very close to my heart. I say this because any time I have to deal with suffering children, be it physically, emotionally or both, it moves me like no other situation I have to deal with. Being a sickly child myself, I still to this day remember the lonely nights spent in a hospital that always felt creepy after the sun went down. I am talking about my experience that happened over fifty-nine years ago.

A DEAF BABY IS HEALED

I was in Denver, Colorado, a couple years back when a situation arose that I do not come across very often. A newborn baby, perhaps only a few months old, was brought to me to be prayed for. It was her grandma, not her own mother who was making this request. I found out later that the mother wasn't serving God at the time and it looked like she was somewhat bitter over the fact the baby was born without the ability to hear. As I have stated earlier in the book, I do not pray for anyone without sizing up the situation to find out from God why a sickness or illness has fallen upon the person in front of me. I could feel the love the grandma had for the baby, yet at the same time I sensed a great love for her daughter as well. I felt in my spirit that grandma was hoping with the healing of the baby, her mama would make her way back to the Lord. When I received my specific instructions from heaven on how this healing was to take place, I asked the grandma to hold out the baby and uncover her ears so that I could blow into them right before I would pray a prayer of faith. I knew this would be challenging, because of course you cannot really communicate with the baby, or at least it cannot respond to you with any kinds of words. I remember thinking, how in the world is God going to confirm this? My answer came immediately after the prayer, because without any prompting grandma called out her name. How in the world the baby knew her name, to this day I have not been able to figure it out. But immediately after calling out, the baby, who up to that time wasn't really responding to any kind of voice or noises, turned her head toward her grandma and gave her the biggest loving smile a baby could give. When I saw that, I almost lost it. It took a great effort for me not to cry with the grandma, rejoicing ever so much that her God had just miraculously healed her granddaughter. To this day, as I relive this experience, the tears continue to well up in my eyes and I thank God I have a front row seat to watch the Creator of the universe do only what He can.

THE DIVERS KINDS OF TONGUES

A COMMON ERROR EXPOSED

By definition, the Divers Kinds of Tongues is a supernatural utterance and a message to the **CHURCH** that requires an interpretation. This gift is **NOT** the initial utterance when you receive the baptism of the Holy Ghost. There is so much confusion in the Christian world about this, coming to the conclusion that the Divers Kinds of Tongues is the same experience as the baptism of the Holy Ghost. A closer examination of the Scriptures helps us to understand that they are actually two different experiences, although they sound similarly alike. Receiving the baptism of the Holy Ghost and speaking in other tongues **(DOREA)** is not the Greek word Paul uses in Corinthians to describe the Divers Kinds of Tongues **(CHARISMA)**. Their purpose is different as well, in that **DOREA** is connected to the salvation plan, according to Acts 2:38, and is for personal edification. **CHARISMA,** on the other hand, is a message to the church and must be interpreted.

THE INTERPRETATION OF TONGUES

INTERPRETATION NOT TRANSLATION

This interpretation will in reality give the theme of the message that has just been given in tongues. The message is an interpretation, NOT a translation. When I first got saved and started to experience this in church, I couldn't get my head wrapped around this gift at times because the message given and its interpretation were different in length of time. What I was able to understand later was like an interpreter in court, a person used in this manner during a church service will summarize the message in a way that is most comfortable to them. There are also questions when an interpretation is given to more than one person in the congregation and they compare notes after the service, there is usually a disagreement amongst the two because one interpretation was more eloquent than the other. Be that as it may, there is no one particular way to interpret a message in tongues. The most important factor to be considered is this: interpret the message and God will take care of the rest.

When the Lord began to use me in this manner, I was so afraid to say the wrong thing. I was so insecure in those days and somewhat of a perfectionist, the Lord really had to pretty much conk me on the head for me to deliver the message in English that He wanted the church to hear. After a period of time with much more experience, the emotional moving of my spirit lessened to the point where if the Lord asks me to interpret a message of tongues today, all He needs to do is tap me gently on the shoulder and I will respond accordingly.

THE GREATEST TEMPTATION

The greatest temptation that must be avoided is trying to add to the interpretation more than what the Lord has told you to say. I recall a hilarious moment during a Christmas service. To this day, I do not remember the prophecy in and of itself except for how it ended. Everything being said appeared to be in order until the person prophesying ended the message with, "and have a Merry Christmas and a happy new year!" Of course, the entire congregation burst out in laughter, and although it may not have been directly from God, we do need to be careful not to add more than what we have been told to say.

THE GIFT OF PROPHECY

The Gift of Prophecy is actually broken up into two parts. There is a lower level and a higher level, given to us to be effective in our service to Him.

TWO LEVELS OF PROPHECY

Lower-level Prophecy includes exhortation, uplifting and encouragement. Our greatest preachers and teachers move in this gift so effectively that they can make a one-hour sermon or lesson appear as only fifteen minutes, leaving the congregation spellbound over every word that comes out of their mouths. There is always a great need for lower-level prophecy.

High-level Prophecy, on the other hand, is in actuality history written in advance and foretelling the future. Of the various times I have prophesied over people, the example I will mention next is one of my favorites.

A YOUNG MAN TRIES TO PULL A FAST ONE

Years ago, I was dealing with a young man who was having horrible physical problems. The Lord immediately helped me to understand that these problems, although physical, were really caused by a spiritual problem that needed to be remedied. I told him that the Lord had revealed to me a falling out he had with his mother. In this particular instance, his mother was the aggressor and really provoked the argument that eventually caused a fight so severe that neither of them had talked to each other for years. As the Lord continued to unravel this situation to me, He also was asking the young man to take the high road and make things right with his foul-mouthed mother. Of course, he objected because it really wasn't his fault that the relationship had become so fractured. If she would not have lost her temper and said the things she said, chances are things would have been resolved a lot sooner.

He was adamant that he would not ask her for forgiveness under any circumstances, until out of nowhere his whole demeanor changed. From one moment to the next he calmed down, but then made a statement that made me question why. He said he would be willing to do what I was asking, but it would be impossible because he had lost track of his mom. She had moved from where she had been living in the past and the last telephone number he had for her was disconnected. A look of pride then surfaced, and shortly after he said that as much as he wanted to make things right, it looked like it would not be possible. The Gift of Prophecy fell upon me, and this was what I prophesied to him. "In three days, out of the blue, you will receive a phone call from your mother. You will then have the opportunity to do what I have asked of you, and if so, God will heal you on the spot." He mockingly laughed at the prophecy, telling me that would never happen. Between being rude and disrespectful, he continued to spew his criticisms towards me. When he walked away from me a little bit later, I really didn't think I would hear from him again.

About five days later, I received a phone call from a person I could not recognize. Because he was emotionally distraught and weeping, I could not understand a word he was saying. It wasn't until I threatened to hang up that this man calmed down and I realized it was the young man who I had just prophesied over five days before. I then asked him what happened. With a broken voice he kept on repeating the question, "How did you know?" I stopped him long enough to utter my question to him, "So what happened?" Again he got very emotional and said everything happened exactly the way I said it would. He received a phone call from his mom, and initially he was going to hang up until in his spirit he kept on hearing my voice in his head, telling him this was the moment to not only make things right, but with that, God would heal him. In his obedience, he asked his mom to forgive him and immediately the glory of the Lord fell upon him, healing him on the spot. Even then he knew he needed to do one more thing, and that was to make things right with me. Never in his wildest imagination did he believe the outcome he was experiencing was possible. Then again, prophetic ministry allows the impossible to find its way into the lives of those who do not believe.

GROUPING THE GIFTS OF THE SPIRIT (DIAGRAM)

We can now take the time to review what we have learned about the gifts of the Spirit and how to categorize them. The boxes below will give a better understanding of what God has established in the spirit world.

Think Like God		
Word of Knowledge	Discerning of Spirits	Word of Wisdom

Act Like God		
Faith	Gifts of Healings	Working of Miracles

Speak Like God		
Divers Kinds of Tongues	Interpretation of Tongues	Prophecy

For the gifts and calling of God are without repentance.

(Romans 11:29)

Whenever I go to a church for the first time and people observe the manner in which I minister in the Gifts of the Spirit, it not only draws a lot of questions but also desires from many who would like to move in that same realm. They are fascinated by the ease in which the miracles are performed, almost as if God Himself was performing them (which He really is). As a matter of fact, the Lord does not allow people to peer into my heart and thought processes, because if that were to be the case, they would find out that most of the time I am ministering, I'm scared half to death. In my experiences watching people who are great at what they do, it is a lot more complicated than how it appears. Talented and gifted people can make the most complex tasks look easy, giving a false impression to those looking on that they too could probably do the same with the same results. There is a lot more to obtaining a powerful gifted ministry than meets the eye. The Scriptures below verify what I have just written. Working in the gifts of the Spirit is not a job, but rather a calling, and if people are not called to this ministry, they are barking up the wrong tree. If you were to ask the sons of Sceva, they too would be able to confirm this. Look what happened to them after they mimicked the ministry of the apostle Paul.

THE GIFTS ARE NOT FOR SHOW

Then some of the itinerant Jewish exorcists took it upon themselves to call the name of the Lord Jesus over those who had evil spirits, saying, "We exorcise you by the Jesus whom Paul preaches." Also there were seven sons of Sceva, a Jewish chief priest, who did so. And the evil spirit answered and said, "Jesus I know, and Paul I know; but who are you?" Then the man in whom the evil spirit was leaped on them, overpowered them, and prevailed against them, so that they fled out that house naked and wounded.

(Acts 19:13-16)

The difference between becoming an expert in the physical realm and gaining an expertise in the spiritual realm is that if in the former, deciding to quit after everything becomes old hat or goes sour, you can depart without it being a capital offense. As to doing the same in the spiritual realm, the consequences can prove to be fatal if the Lord chooses to take you out instead of taking away that gift.

> *Every branch in Me that does not bear fruit He takes away; and every branch that bears fruit He prunes, that it may bear more fruit.*
>
> *(John 15:2)*

On the other hand, I have seen backslidden servants of God continue to minister powerfully without demonstrating any drop off in their success, while at the same time living in sin, committing adultery, dabbling in pornography, embezzling church finances, intimidating their congregation, etc. Has the Lord gone soft in this last generation? The answer is a resounding no, which can be explained by Scripture we find in Matthew 7:21-23:

"Not everyone who says to Me, 'Lord, Lord,' Shall enter the kingdom of heaven, but he who does the will of My Father in heaven. Many will say to Me in that day, 'Lord, Lord, have we not prophesied in Your name, cast out demons in Your name, and done many wonders in Your name?' And then I will declare to them, 'I never knew you; depart from Me, you who practice lawlessness!'"

Practicing lawlessness means that in order to be successful in this life, following the law can at times be circumvented. This train of thought leads to a belief that "the end always justifies the means," no matter where that would lead you. That may work in a world apart from God, notwithstanding, keeping the law of God brings blessing into the lives of those who obey it.

Keep my commands and live, and my law
as the apple of your eye.

(Proverbs 7:2)

The phrase, "apple of your eye" refers to something or someone that one cherishes above all others. The commandments of God cannot be altered, adjusted, adapted, amended, modified, or revised to fit our agenda. These instructions were given to us to follow as is without second-guessing God's word. Jesus adamantly told us, *"If you love Me, keep My commandments."* (John 14:15)

KING CYRUS: GOD'S SERVANT

As difficult as it is to reconcile this Scripture with disobedient, sinful servants of God, let me strengthen the argument with the example of King Cyrus in the Old Testament. He was a heathen king who knew not the Lord. Isaiah was instructed to write this about him:

"Thus says the Lord to His anointed, to Cyrus, whose right hand I have held—to subdue nations before him and loose the armor of kings, to open before him the double doors, so that the gates will not be shut: I will go before you and make the crooked places straight; I will break in pieces the gates of bronze and cut the bars of iron. I will give you the treasures of darkness and hidden riches of secret places, that you may know that I, the Lord, who call you by your name, Am the God of Israel.

(Isaiah 45:1-3)

The Lord actually used this heathen to cause Israel to repent and humbly return to the Lord. Does that mean King Cyrus was admitted into heaven regardless of his sinful life? I doubt it, because sin is sin and "The soul who sins will die" (Ezekiel 18:20). If a sinner is all God has to work with to bring judgment to His children, this is a great example of that fact.

HOW TO GET STARTED

Every good gift and every perfect gift is from above, and comes down from the Father of lights, with whom there is no variation or shadow of turning.

(James 1:17)

SEEK GOD NOT THE GIFTS

The questions I am asked the most are these, "How did you get started ministering like you do and is it possible for anyone to do it as well?" When I give the answer to them, most of the time they are taken aback because it's difficult for them to believe what I have said is true. I have always told anybody who asks and is willing to listen that first of all, I never asked for any of the gifting God has given to me. Shortly after I was saved, I was having a difficult time finding my place in God. I have mentioned this in prior books that I honestly believed God had made a mistake in calling me because I had none of the natural attributes given to most people that would allow me to be a successful minister. I was not a natural born leader with a charismatic personality. I was considered more on the shy side, somewhat quiet and withdrawn. I was not a people person and was quite content playing "follow the leader." At the same time, a burning desire to be used by God was overwhelming and I just couldn't reconcile the paradox that I was. The only way I could escape my uneasiness in my Christian walk was to escape into the presence of God, spending hours at a time, feeling more comfortable there than anywhere else. I became a magnificent worshiper and my time spent in His presence meant more to me than anything else. Unbeknownst to me, I was building a foundation in the miraculous to be used by God, without even knowing it. My relationship with Him not only stirred my soul, but it also opened the door for me to allow the Lord to trust me with His secrets. That is how it all started, and to this day continues to grow by His grace.

Anyone who has been successful in any area of life, spiritual or not, has always had someone take them under their wing and share what they have learned and experienced. In my case, that person is Evangelist Freddy Clark from Rocky Mount, Virginia. Up to that point in my life (early forties) I had never seen anyone used by God in the way the Lord uses Bro. Freddy. The Word of Knowledge, Word of Wisdom, Gifts of Healings, Working of Miracles, and Gift of Faith flowed so freely and so powerfully, I remember wondering to myself why more men and women of God did not allow God to use them in this same manner. Truth be told, most people are not living the Christian life they portray to others, and if found out would be called out to be what they really are, hypocrites and frauds.

I then attended one of his three-day seminars and have never been the same since. Although I had been prayed over to receive the two gifts I had asked God for, it appeared my faith was not great enough to launch out with the faith I needed to be successful. Because I was not willing to minister exactly in the manner of my mentor, I made an adjustment in the way I would minister that would allow me to take baby steps. Instead of calling various diseases out in public, I began whispering in the ear of those I was ministering to. It was at that moment the Lord began to distinguish my healing ministry from that of Bro. Clark. The strength of my ministry now using the Word of Knowledge helps me to secretly deal with emotional and/or spiritual problems without shamelessly humiliating those in need. These are the types of problems that, if announced in public, would cause total embarrassment to the person I would be trying to help. It is not as dynamic as the old school way of the past, but on the other hand it makes things so much easier for the person suffering to be set free. Why is this important? First and foremost, we have not been gifted to put on a show. Ministering in the Gifts was meant to heal and set the captives free, not glorify or puff up the gifted person ministering.

PRACTICE, PRACTICE, PRACTICE

Now, in order to become successful in your gifting, you need to know how your gift or gifts will function. The only way you will be able to know this is through PRACTICE. That means you will enter into a period of trial and error, one which will test your courage to carry on and to see if you have the heart to follow through when the going gets tough. With much practice, after a while a pattern will form, and you can depend on it. Sometimes, a pattern doesn't have to necessarily form, in that once you know what type of disease or illness it is and what has caused it, this immediately allows your faith to skyrocket into a higher level. This has happened to me every time I deal with people suffering from fibromyalgia. Once I hear that disease called out, my faith is turbocharged to the point I have no doubt that person will be healed. I would estimate out of the fifty people, more or less, I have prayed for, only two have not been healed instantly of this disease.

PAYBACK

There is one more connection I would like to make about my particular healing ministry that I cannot prove biblically, but it makes a lot of sense to me. When I had polio as a five-year-old, one of the issues I had to deal with was a crooked spine. Even after being miraculously healed by the Lord, I was told I had to wear a body cast to help straighten out my spine. It was a removable cast made of plaster (today I believe they are made out of hard plastic), and it was my body armor until I went to sleep at night. Mentioning this is important, because any time I have to deal with people with back problems, whether spinal stenosis, spina bifida, bulging discs, pinched nerves, osteoporosis, sciatica, etc., they almost always heal. I believe it is payback to Satan, who tried to kill me at the age of five, which of course did not work.

One of the greatest lessons I have learned in using the Gifts of the Spirit is that according to James 1:17, every good and perfect gift comes from God. How successful those gifts are depends on the person that good gift has fallen upon. In other words, our gifting in God will vary in type, in intensity, and in purpose according to His will.

However, our God always comes through and our God does not change. He is the same yesterday, today, and forever!

How exactly do we receive our gifting and how does it grow to become effective?

THE SEED IS IN ITSELF

The fruit tree yielding fruit after his kind, whose seed is in itself...

(Genesis 1:11)

The Lord leaves us a great example of how our gifting is perfected. It begins in seed form, which comes from the fruit itself. Once a fruit tree produces its fruit, the seeds from that fruit can be replanted to grow another tree, which in turn will bear more fruit. The seed of the gift comes out of the gift itself, consequently every gifted person you sit under gives you the possibility to duplicate that gift. For instance, haven't you ever noticed that churches pastored by a great preacher produce great preachers as well? Why is it that churches with a great music ministry, whether singers, musicians, or both, seem to reproduce themselves with another generation of great music ministers? Finally, a pastor who gives generously to missions will always produce a congregation of givers as it becomes second nature for them to give sacrificially because they understand the blessings that are returned to them in abundance. Finally, laying hands on someone will not necessarily give that someone a gift of the Spirit, it only packs the soil of the seed that has been planted, ordaining and commissioning that seed to grow.

As you continue to grow in your gifting, you will find distinct signs that will follow you.

And these signs will follow those who believe: In My name they will cast out demons; they will speak with new tongues; they will take up serpents; and if they drink anything deadly, it will by no means hurt them; they will lay hands on the sick, and they will recover.

(Mark 16:17-18)

Early in the use of my gifting, because of a lack of experience and faith, I chose the safe path by copying word-for-word and step-by-step the things my mentor successfully used in his ministry. I soon found out, after failing miserably, the Lord was willing to give me my own unique signs to help me gain my confidence in Him. Like I mentioned earlier, whereas the strength of Freddy Clark's ministry is in physical healing, what I hang my hat on today is dealing with emotional and spiritual problems, whispering in their ear so that there is no embarrassment or guilt that would hinder the healing process.

EXAMPLES OF SIGNS

The Lord uses signs that turn out to be the proof that the healing is taking or has taken place. For example:

- The removal of pain
- The removal of stiffness, lumps, or growths
- Full body heat is a sign of blood transfusion
- Isolated spot of heat shows that spot is being healed
- After the spirit of nicotine is cast out, the nicotine taste is gone
- After the spirit of alcoholism is cast out, the smell of alcohol leaves
- A heart flutter is revealed by a vision of a butterfly

- Pulling an imaginary string out of a throat heals throat conditions
- A whole-body x-ray reveals pain in certain areas of the body
- Blow into deaf ears and they will open up
- Partial healing is a sign God is not done yet
- Spiritual amnesia erases memory of past sins
- Oil on the palm of the hands is a sign of a special anointing
- Calling out specific names
- Dealing with pain on the left side of the body

Of all the different signs listed above, I would like to choose three of them to give you an example and give you in greater detail how God blesses in His kingdom.

A SIGN I WILL NEVER FORGET

The first time I ever saw Evangelist Freddy Clark minister there were so many things he did that evening, I could not wrap my head around most of them. But there was one thing he did that I will never, ever forget. Although the service had gone on extremely long and most of the people had already left, he did something I had never seen before. He had a young lady raise her hands and then asked the question, "Sister, have you been asking God for an anointing?" As she nodded her head yes, he then responded with these words. "Hold out your hands and look at them." To her amazement, her hands were dripping with oil. He then said, "Don't touch them," and proceeded to show the pastor her hands as proof of what God had just done. He then scraped oil off one palm and walked to the other end of the sanctuary and began anointing people with the oil on his hands. I was somewhat dismayed, because we were on the other end of the building and I knew there would not be enough oil left for us. He continued to anoint and pray over each person, and when he finally got to me about 200 people later, he still had oil flowing from his hand. From that night forward, I had an unexpected anointing that I believe I still have in my ministry, and it appears to be getting stronger.

GOD CALLS HER NAME: ROSE

There was another instance while preaching a revival, I saw God do something extraordinary the first two nights of that meeting. A member of the local church was evangelizing a woman who had been strung out on drugs. No matter how hard in the past she tried to get free, she always fell back to what had her bound for years. I really don't remember the message I preached that night, but it did have some effect on her because although she walked into church high as a kite, the prayer made for her set her free. Although she had made a decision never to use drugs again, she was greatly aware of the fact she would have to go through withdrawals. She went on that night preparing for the worst, but the worst never came. She woke up the next day completely sober, and she was so appreciative of the miracle God had done in her life, she wanted to go back to church that evening to show that appreciation. Personally, not knowing what had happened, in preparing for the evening service, the Lord placed in my mind to preach a message entitled, "Let It Unfold." It included the poem seen next. Little did I know the great impact it would have on her. Here it is:

Unfolding the Rosebud
By Pastor Darryl L. Brown.

It is only a tiny rosebud,
A flower of God's design;
But I cannot unfold the petals
With these clumsy hands of mine.
The secret of unfolding flowers
Is not known to such as I.
GOD opens this flower so sweetly,
When in my hands they fade and die.

If I cannot unfold a rosebud,
This flower of God's design,
Then how can I think I have wisdom
To unfold this life of mine?

So I'll trust in Him for His leading
Each moment of every day.
I will look to Him for His guidance
Each step of the pilgrim way.

The pathway that lies before me,
Only my Heavenly Father knows.
I'll trust Him to unfold the moments,
Just as He unfolds the rose.

As I made my way through the message, she was overly moved by the word of God. In actuality, it was the reading of the poem at various times in the message that broke her completely. Crying without any reservation by the time I was done, she came to the altar and God filled her with the baptism of the Holy Ghost, speaking in tongues for the first time. I found out later it wasn't so much my preaching that moved her, it had more to do with the poem because she had taken it personally. Why did it have such an impact on her? Her name was Rose. In reaching out to find a better life, the Lord knew where to send her so that He could speak to her directly and have her understand that although she had lived a miserable life, one that hardly anyone cared about, the Lord had been waiting for her just so that He could call her by name.

THE MOST BEAUTIFUL TONGUES I HAVE EVER HEARD

The last testimony happened earlier this year (2019) while ministering in Canada. Because I was not familiar with the country, our scheduled visits were really far apart. On one of the Saturdays we had to check out of our hotel by noon and our service that day did not start until

6:30 PM. The drive that day was about 2 ½ hours away. We waited in the car until service started and were not done ministering until midnight. We then drove another two hours to the city where we would be ministering on Sunday. Finally getting to sleep about 2:30 AM, I woke up at 6 AM to prepare for the morning service. We hurried things up to arrive at our next destination, which was another two hours away, trying to rest up enough to have the strength to finish the day. I couldn't shake off the tiredness until something miraculous happened. Out of nowhere, a breeze my wife and I believe was angels brought relief to our tired bodies and immediately snapped me out of my tiredness. There was no other way to explain it because there were no doors open to allow that breeze to refresh us. I was able to preach, but then that same tiredness came upon me again. Because of a lack of time, we were only able to minister to one young lady who had a great desire to receive the Holy Ghost. Because of her hesitance to deal with us, I asked the pastor before we began to pray for the Holy Ghost if he could take some time to calm her down. As he and his wife took over, something amazing happened. With her nerves calmed, she began to worship God, and a short time later she broke out speaking in other tongues. I marveled at what was going on because the languages (yes, more than one) were the most beautiful thing I had ever heard. I could have sworn that there were some words being spoken that I could understand and yet most of what she was saying was not understandable. When she finally calmed down and thanked us, I made a comment about how beautiful she was speaking, in a way I had never experienced before. She then said this, which blew me away: "I had asked the Lord when He filled me with His Spirit, I wanted to speak in French, Italian, and Portuguese." After hearing those words, I understood why I was able to understand some of what she was saying. Just when I thought I had seen it all, the Lord through His Spirit does something to surprise me.

DEALING WITH CANCER

I left dealing with cancer till the end because it needs to be dealt with somewhat differently from the other diseases. Cancer is a curse and is a spirit because it is attached to the bloodstream and life is in the blood (Deuteronomy 12:23). If your spirit can live in your body, then other spirits can as well. The enemy can attack your body because we have not yet been glorified, but cancer cannot reach the eternal part of you. Rest assured that your body may die, but cancer cannot kill your soul.

Because cancer is a spirit, you have to cast out that spirit before you can curse the cancer. You cannot beat cancer by willing it to go away. Once a spirit is cast out, you must do three things to maintain your healing:

1. Thank God

Oh, give thanks to the Lord, for He is good! For His mercy endures forever.

(Psalm 118:29)

2. Testify

Come and hear, all you who fear God, and I will declare what He has done for my soul.

(Psalm 66:16)

3. Rebuke the devil

"And the Lord said to Satan! "The Lord who has chosen Jerusalem rebuke you!

(Zechariah 3:2)

CASTING SATAN INTO THE DEEP

When the unclean spirit is gone out of a man, he walks through dry places, seeking rest; and finding none, he says, I will return unto my house where I came out.

(Luke 11:24)

Because Satan actually does his best work in dry places, it is counterproductive to send him there. It is a place where he rests and we should cast him out of his comfort zone and send him to the deep where the corridors of hell are (the lowest part of the earth). Once sent to the deep, the demon spirit cannot return to dry places. That is the reason why Legion did not want to be sent to the deep to be judged and preferred a place where they could live. Once inside the pigs, the pigs themselves committed suicide by drowning in the water.

> *Then the demons went out of the man and entered the swine, and the herd ran violently down the steep place into the lake and drowned.*
>
> *(Luke 8:33)*

Once a spirit is sent to the deep, it goes to the door in the lower region of the condemned, then to the corridor in the lake of fire that is in the center of the earth. Most scientists will tell you the center of the earth is a molten fire.

HOW GOD HAS USED WATER THROUGH HISTORY

Throughout eternity, the Lord has used water effectively to do His will:

Water was used as a judgment when Lucifer was kicked out of heaven and the whole earth was flooded.

The earth was without form, and void; and darkness was on the face of the deep. And the Spirit of God was hovering over the face of the waters.

(Genesis 1:2)

Water was present when Jesus died on Calvary.

But one of the soldiers pierced His side with a spear, and immediately blood and water came out.

(John 19:34)

Water is an essential part of salvation.

Jesus answered, "Most assuredly, I say to you, unless one is born of water and the Spirit, he cannot enter the kingdom of God."

(John 3:5)

CASTING OUT A SPIRIT OF CANCER

Every spirit is likened to the god he serves, grotesque and perverted. If you take the spirit out of the body where the tumor lies, it will eventually show signs of death. You have to cast out the life of that disease first before the process begins. More times than not, it will not disappear immediately, but in time it'll fall off, die, be absorbed in the bloodstream or through the pores. It is very similar to the process that the body goes through when a scab is healing. Little by little it begins to fall off and eventually it's completely gone. Do not be intimidated by what you don't see. There are things going on in the spiritual realm that are not visible to the naked eye. Nevertheless, God's promises are true and we must stick to our guns when there is no visible confirmation.

I am still in the learning stages of dealing with cancer. There have been times in the past when I have dealt with this disease as any other. There were times where people were healed and other times nothing happened. It was such a hit and miss experience for me that it was very difficult to gain any traction in the understanding of how to deal with cancer.

Recently, I dealt with two women who lived 1,200 miles apart. Both had stage IV cancer in the same area (the stomach). One of them was in her early thirties while the other one was in her sixties. I ministered to the younger one in her local church and with a Word of Knowledge the Lord revealed to me where the root of the problem was. It lay in her marriage and how she was reacting to being verbally abused. When I whispered in her ear what I was sensing in the Spirit, she broke down crying, admitting that it was true. While the altar call was going on, I took them each, husband and wife, and told them what needed to be done to be healed. Because of time constraints, I'm not sure if they followed my instructions or not.

Sad to say, she died several months later, leaving behind her school-age children.

On the other hand, the sixty-year-old woman was dealt with completely differently. The tumor was in the same area, but my instructions to her did not come anywhere near what I did in dealing with the younger woman. I told her that when we prayed, she would vomit up the tumor and that everything would be okay. As the family got together to pray, I could sense in my spirit that there was a lot of doubt and uncertainty over what I had prophesied. Nevertheless, when I prayed for her, she began to vomit. The weird thing about this occurrence was that she still needed to go through chemo and several months later was pronounced "cancer-free." Relieved that everything was okay, she was shocked when several months later the cancer came back. We recently went back and prayed for her and are believing God for the best. Each case is different, and unless there are many people dealt with, trying to find a pattern for ultimate success is a slow process. I am waiting for the day when dealing with cancer-ridden people that I will have the same success rate and confidence dealing with this "killer" in the same manner that

I deal with fibromyalgia. For whatever reasons, when I pray for people with this particular disease, they heal about 99 percent of the time.

EPILOGUE

Nevertheless do not rejoice in this, that the spirits are subject to you, but rather rejoice because your names are written in heaven.

(Luke 10:20)

The church of today is so enamored with hoopla that it has taken center stage in our worship services. It has become more of an avenue of entertainment, sensationalizing every move that is made to bring enjoyment to the congregation. As the Lord begins to convince the church of today of the importance of using the Gifts of the Spirit to win souls, there are those who will stray from the focus for evangelism and substitute it for "an ooh and aah" experience.

There are others who will not use this "gifting" in the manner God had intended it to be used. Taking the lead from the New Testament Corinthian church, using the gifts without discipline and holiness, the church of today is mixing godliness with worldliness. Like Corinth, we believe that the end justifies the means, and if we are not being judged for such lawlessness, then it must not be that bad. We must not make the same mistake. Let us rally together in this last hour, evangelizing the lost world, hitting the streets armed with the "Gifts of the Spirit."

George Pantages Ministries
Books Available in English

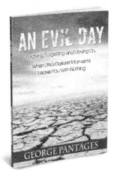 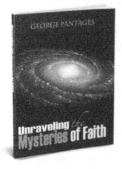 

 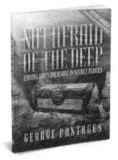 

"Thanks for reading! If you enjoyed this book or found it useful, I'd be very grateful if you'd post a short review on Amazon. Your support really does make a difference.

Thanks again for your support!"

George Pantages Ministries
Libros Disponibles en Español

 George Pantages Ministries
Cell 512-785-6324
GEOPANJR@YAHOO.COM

Made in the USA
Monee, IL
18 May 2025

17498565R00115